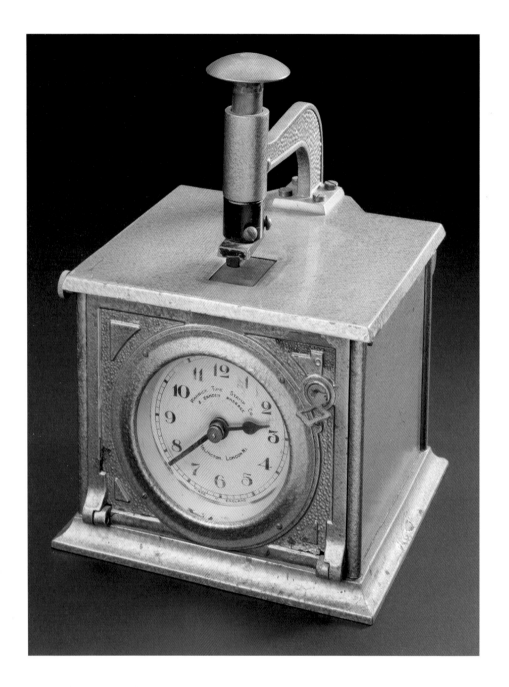

Warwick Time Stamp Co., *Time Recorder*, ca.1890

24/7: A WAKE-UP CALL FOR OUR NON-STOP WORLD

Edited by Sarah Cook

PAINS,	No. XII. PAINS,			
N.	—of LABOUR—toil—fatigue.			
	Corresponding Interest,			
	Interest of the PILLOW.			
NAMES,	Corresponding MOTIVES—with NAMES,			
—III. DYSLOGISTIC.	—I. NEUTRAL. Single-worded, none.	—II. EULOGISTIC. None.	—III. DYSLOGISTIC.	
on. &c.—piety, &c.—as above, Col. 2.	Many-worded,		1. Indolence.	9. Listlessness.
8. Religious prejudice.	1. Love of ease.		2. Laziness.	10. Torpidness.
n. 9. Religious frenzy.	2. Aversion to labour.		3. Sloth.	11. Torpidity.
10. Religious intolerance.	3. Fear, apprehension, dread—of toil, fatigue, over-exertion, over-working, over-straining.		4. Slothfulness.	12. Segnity.
iousness.			5. Sluggardliness.	
			6. Sluggishness.	13. Tardiness.
of, pre-			7. Self-indulgence.	14. Dilatoriness.
—religion,			8. Idleness.	15. Procrastination.
				16. Slowness.
				17. Lenitude.
PAINS,				18. Drawlingness.

No. XIII. PAINS,

—of DEATH, and BODILY Pains in general.

Corresponding Interest

, comprehensive—in proportion to

Jeremy Bentham, *A Table of the Springs of Action: shewing the several species of pleasures and pains, of which man's nature is susceptible: together with the several species of interests, desires, and motives, respectively corresponding to them:...* (detail), 1817

CONTENTS

Marcus Coates, *Self Portrait as Time*, 2016

FOREWORD

Sarah Cook and Jonathan Reekie

Tired all the time? Can't log-off? Did you sleep last night? I'm shattered... what about you?

The book, *24/7*, by art historian and essayist Jonathan Crary, which describes our shared condition of unrest, was the starting point for this exhibition of the same name. In the book, first published in 2013[1], a light is shone on the way we've come to live in a culture in which we consume content via the screen at all hours of the day and night, and our every interaction is tracked, mined, and predicted. Crary's evocation of sleep, and time spent dreaming, as the last preserve of our lives which hasn't yet been parcelled up and sold back to us as commodities (despite there being lavender pillow sprays for sale with packaging which reads

1. And others published since, such as *Infinite Distraction* (2016) by Dominic Pettman; *Insomnia* (2018) by Marina Benjamin; *New Dark Age* (2018) by James Bridle; *Surveillance Capitalism* (2019) by Shoshana Zuboff to name a handful. A list of further reading is included at the end of this book.

'choose sleep'), is a powerful and unsettling vision:

> In its profound uselessness and intrinsic passivity, with the incalculable losses it causes in production time, circulation, and consumption, sleep will always collide with the demands of a 24/7 universe. The huge portion of our lives that we spend asleep, freed from a morass of simulated needs, subsists as one of the great human affronts to the voraciousness of contemporary capitalism.[2]

As you read the book, with its beguiling descriptions of film works and art – Joseph Wright of Derby's paintings (ca.1770–1790s), Chantal Akerman's *D'Est* (1993), Chris Marker's *La Jetée* (1962) – an exhibition begins to form in the mind. The text's vivid descriptions of the numerous overlapping conditions that have enabled the 24/7 universe also evokes an Instagram-like endless scroll of works by artists and designers grappling today with these complexities – of rampant capitalism, automation, acceleration, distraction, surveillance and *sousveillance*. Artists have long been bellwethers for our changing relationships to time, to place, to how we live and work, as well as to the technologies themselves which reconfigure those anew – whether it's a camera, a wifi network, a drone, or an algorithm. Even with an action as simple as turning the lights on and off, artists can show us not just the shape and structure of the times we inhabit (and structures of time management which we rail against) but also other times we could inhabit and reconfigure our working and waking lives around. In the Afterword to this book Crary reminds us that as we try and make sense of our world, we need to pay attention to what artists are interrogating.

2. Jonathan Crary, *24/7: Late Capitalism and the Ends of Sleep* (New York; London: Verso, 2014) p.10.

Joseph Wright of Derby, *Arkwright's Cotton Mills by Night*, ca.1790s

Rut Blees Luxemburg, *A Modern Project (Highrise),* 1995
C-type on Aluminium, 60 × 75 cm

Sleep is both a metaphor for logging off (your device has a sleep mode) but it is also a real thing we absolutely need to survive. Poor sleep is a public health epidemic, and while an exhibition cannot single-handedly solve that, despite one brilliantly challenging proposal from an artist to geoengineer the genes of plants to release sleep-inducing molecules into the air[3], we know there isn't a quick fix. Discovering solutions to this epidemic is going to take all of us changing our ways, possibly by remembering old ways. Exhibitions are useful, however, as shared social occasions at which to reflect, and reconsider, to face up to complex problems in the here and now, so that we, together, might think differently about them as we step out of the door into the cold light of day. As Crary puts it, into 'an illuminated world without shadows'.

We anticipate that every visitor to the show will find their own pace through the works on view.[4] Some of the works are positioned in order to be experienced with others.

3. Tega Brain is developing this work with Elizabeth Henaff, in the spirit of other current planet-wide geoengineering non-art works designed with the opposite effect in mind, such as spraying particles in the upper atmosphere to reflect sunlight, or launching satellites to act as artificial moons to light cities at night (Chengdu www.theguardian. com/science/2018/oct/17/chinese-city-plans-to-launch-artificial-moon-to-replace-streetlights). These continued to capture our attention as we developed the checklist for the exhibition.

4. In pulling together a list for this exhibition, we veered away from solely digital media and considered many historic works of art – as well as of literature, design, film, and popular culture – which sit in a continuation of conversation with the many media art works exhibited. The longer list considered how artists mark the passing of time, how they work or perform labour, and how they relate to natural and artificial cycles of light. (It's endless, but those visual artists whose action-based works continue to scroll in our heads include, for example, Otto Piene; Hanne Darboven; Andy Warhol; On Kawara; Mierle Laderman Ukeles; Tehching Hsieh...).

Are as far as H the same as in the plan excepting
only F which does not appear.

I annular cistern for water to supply every cell.	&c ct for keeping provisions tools & materials	to ventilate the whole building when opened.
K Rooms serving for lodging the taskmasters, inspector	L Large annular sky light, serving	M Skylight to the Chapel. N.O Parts not yet applied to any use.

Plan of House of Inspection.

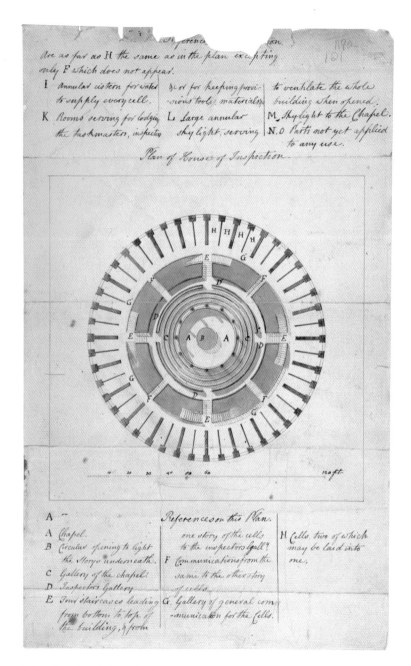

A ‑	References on this Plan.	
A Chapel.	one story of the cells	H Cells, two of which
B Circular opening to light the storys underneath.	to the inspectors gall? F Communications from the	may be laid into one.
C Gallery of the chapel.	same to the other story	
D Inspectors Gallery	of cells.	
E Four staircases leading from bottom to top of the building, & from	G Gallery of general communication for the cells.	

Some are humorous diversions, while others are restorative. We have grouped the works – all of which draw attention to our 'clockwork condition'[5] – into five sections (an exhibition object list appears at the end of this book), although the interconnectedness of the triggers and tensions present in our 24/7 lives make this far from a neat linear narrative. Additional navigation is enabled by Lucy Carter's lighting design that aims to reflect the circadian rhythms of a 24-hour cycle of night and day, dawn and dusk.

In notes for her book, *How to Do Nothing* (2019), artist Jenny Odell argues that,

> In a situation where every waking moment has become pertinent to our making a living, and when we submit even our leisure for numerical evaluation via likes on Facebook and Instagram, constantly checking on its performance like one checks a stock, monitoring the ongoing development of our personal brand, time becomes an economic resource that we can no longer justify spending on 'nothing.' It provides no return on investment; it is simply too expensive.[6]

Doing nothing is a privilege not many of us have, and apathy is not what our world needs right now either. There is a

5. *The Clockwork Condition* is the title of an unfinished manuscript by Anthony Burgess, a follow-up to *A Clockwork Orange*, the discovery of which, by Prof Andrew Biswell, was announced during preparations for the exhibition. It is reportedly a treatise on 'the contemporary human condition' including sections on 'the possible corrupting effects of visual culture' and 'the bland neutrality' of mechanised life in the 1970s.
6. Jenny Odell, 'Notes from How to Do Nothing', transcript of a talk given at EYEO 2017 in Minneapolis, available, www.medium.com/@the_jennitaur/how-to-do-nothing-57e100f59bbb

further paradox in this for designers and artists who work creatively and challengingly with digital media at a time when digital media is often blamed for the relentlessness of our lives. This anxiety is shared by cultural workers creating experiences for broadly understood 'audiences'. Who has time to engage with the content we're curating, and the things artists are making? Odell, and the essayists we invited to write for this book, point out this contradiction. Doing nothing might be an action of refusal at an individual level, but are we too complacent about what is needed to change our 24/7 condition at the collective level? The essays published here all argue for practising a different kind of attention – whether that is to the way we use our devices (as Esther Leslie argues), or to the spaces we share together (as Malcolm McCullough describes), or to one other (as Dominic Smith reflects on). Therefore, researching and curating *24/7*, has been an effort in sustaining attention, both upon the conditions enabling our distracted and overtired states, and to the question of what – societally, politically, personally – is at risk, from us 'paying' attention to whatever-capitalist-consumerist-rubbish-entertaining-enlightening-video-audio-animation-photograph-piece-of-junk we are giving our attention to for free at the expense of our rest/sleep.

Distributing our attention as a precious and limited resource takes stamina and commitment. Douglas Coupland's essay says that without fail he keeps a set number of hours for sleep, and attributes whatever modicum of success he has in his life to maintaining this routine. In developing the exhibition and this accompanying publication we nevertheless had to work around the clock, for example, FaceTiming with artists in other time zones (such as Douglas Coupland) when we had just woken up and they were about to go to sleep, or vice versa – befitting the theme of the project.

Tatsuo Miyajima, *Life Palace (tea room)*, 2013. L.E.D., IC, microcomputer by Ikegami program, wood, steel, passive sensor, electric wire, LED type; Life G-BL 152 pieces, 258.8 × 321.6 × 321.6 cm, 101 7/8 × 126 5/8 × 126 5/8 in

Ultimately the aim of the exhibition is to reflect, as Crary suggests, that perhaps we all need a new dream, 'one dream, superseding all others, [...] of a shared world whose fate is not terminal, a world without billionaires, which has a future other than barbarism or the post-human, and in which history can take on other forms than reified nightmares of catastrophe.'[7]

How do we give shape to that dream? What cultural conditions are needed? What behaviours wrought by technology – whether clocks or computers – and habituated to cycles of working and wakefulness, should be relinquished?

Much of the thinking about tuning out and turning off is not about abdicating responsibility to fight the systems, but a call to action which starts by recognising the challenges, and creating regular, recurrent routines which might resist or impede them. If it becomes a habit to check Twitter as soon as we open our eyes, it will also take a new habit – yoga? Sex? Okay, how about just leaving the devices out of the bedroom? – to break out of that routine. Odell again writes,

> the artist creates a structure – whether that's a map or a cordoned-off area – that holds open a contemplative space against the pressures of habit and familiarity that constantly threaten to close it.[8]

It is for these reasons that this book includes instinctive (time-delimited) replies from Somerset House Studios'

7. *24/7*, op. cit., p.128.
8. 'Notes from How to Do Nothing', op. cit.

resident artists and designers to questions about how they keep time, what is stealing their attention and what art has to do with any of this. Their answers speak to the potential of art – and longer-term, research-driven projects like this one – to articulate problems, to alter perspectives, to slow us down, and set new rhythms of response which might lead us to rethink the value of 'timeliness' altogether. It turns out that making and viewing art, and giving our collective time and attention to a creative and cultural commons, could be, like sleep, itself a shared form of resistance.

September 2019, London – Dundee – Glasgow and points inbetween

Sarah Cook is Professor at the University of Glasgow in Information Studies and Curator with NEoN Digital Arts Festival, Dundee.

Jonathan Reekie CBE is the Director of Somerset House Trust.

Alan Warburton, *Sprites I* & *IV*, 2016

SHOPPING WHILE SLEEPING IS A FASCINATING IDEA

Douglas Coupland, *Slogans for the 21st Century,* 2011–ongoing

IN YOUR DREAMS

Douglas Coupland

This year I flew to Auckland on Air New Zealand and unlike most other airlines, it has wifi that not only works – it's insanely fast and good, even in the middle of the Pacific. I asked a flight attendant why they had it, and she replied that it was a way of making time pass more quickly and that passengers were generally far more sedated when they have wifi, and they prefer it to sleeping. I find this a useful metaphor for modern existence and the way we experience time. A thousand years ago we mostly lived in mud huts and forts. The word 'future' didn't exist. Why would it? People lived entirely in the present; what few stories there were to remind them of 'the past' were called myths and fuzzily transmitted forward. Our brains received three-and-a-half dopamine hits a week, and we lived in a perpetual foggy present. If we were in an up-scale part of the world, the only music in our lives might be a church bell, which was basically the internet of AD 1019. A thousand years later, we receive hundreds, thousands, of dopamine hits a *day*. The part of our brain that regulates our time perception has been overloaded and exhausted, causing our sense of past, present and future to melt together. There is no past; the future turns into the present so quickly that it no longer exists. Ten years ago feels like ten minutes ago. What, it's 2020 already? A friend of mine works at FitBit in California, the company that makes wrist devices that measure how many steps you took that day; how much you slept; how much of that was deep and shallow sleep, your REM cycles and I'm guessing pretty much everything else about you. I asked him what kinds of things a FitBit can tell me about my sleep. He replied, 'The best thing I can do is send you a Fitbit to wear for a while. You can track your sleep (REM/ Light Sleep/Deep Sleep etc.) with sensors and algorithms. It gives you a good idea of dreams vs reality ratio.' I pause here to reread that last line: *'it gives you a good idea of dreams vs. reality ratio.'*

It seems to me that the only part of our lives where this 21st century neural reconfiguration has had no impact is within our sleeping and dreaming lives. But maybe I'm wrong. But then, what is sleep? What is dreaming? Why do we bother sleeping? Do all animals sleep? People say sharks don't sleep, but I don't buy it. All marine vertebrates have to have a down mode – unless they come from a non-revolving planet with no cyclical daylight over the past billion years. Even fish are now known to 'sing' a dawn chorus. How many hours of sleep do you get per day? I need it. You need it. We all need it.

I'm a sleep freak. I get nine and a half hours every day of my life, and it's why I've been self-employed since 1988 – I've based my entire life on getting those nine and a half hours, and it's why I never do morning radio or TV work or take early flights. Sleep always comes first. My mother has hypothyroidism and sleeps more than anyone I've ever met. When I was in secondary school, she told me that if I ever needed to get more sleep, I could skip class and she'd write me a note – which is an offer I never accepted, which is odd, because now my life revolves around sleep. If I've accomplished anything in this world, it's most likely because of my rigid adherence to getting uncompromised nightly down-time.

Sometimes sleep disturbance can't be avoided, such as with trans-polar air travel. For me it's either from Vancouver (home) to Europe, or Vancouver to Asia, and on these flights – highly unnatural in themselves – I've noticed that there's always that one passenger who leaves their window louvers open during the 'night-time' polar section of these flights, and I think these people are assholes. Whereas most passengers in a cabin are in some form of discomfort while trying to nab what little sleep they can within a craft's badly ventilated and cramped space, the git in 35K pops his shade and wrecks it for everyone, allowing Greenland, 35,000 feet below, to radioactively bathe the plane's interior with gleaming white light. And the thing is, if you ask a flight attendant to do an intervention and see if the asshole in 35K can lower their blind, the flight attendant immediately makes 'the face' – the face that tells you that they know in their bones that before they ask Mr. 35K to lower the louver, the request is doomed. They know the response will be: 'This is my seat and my property, my real estate, so to speak, and I choose to leave my louvers open.' Almost invariably, these passengers have read a scammy unscientific online article about how to plan their travel's sleep architecture: Try melatonin! Leave your window louver open so that your circadian rhythms can shift organically! Why do these people bother me so much? It's because we have so few examples of the common good in our culture of space which is owned, inhabited and politicised so intensely and so entirely in real

ARTIST INTERVIEW

Inés Cámara Leret

Artist combining a critical research practice with scientific rigour and an highly experimental making process.

What is your relationship to 24/7 culture (as evidenced by the ceaselessness of contemporary capitalism)?

'It's complicated'. It is the only system I have lived in, yet I am old enough to have seen and experienced the growth of communication technologies and how they've impacted and become embedded within our culture.

How do you work/sleep/play (keeping in the mind the old adage of '8 hours of work, 8 hours of rest, 8 hours of what we will')?

I had never heard of this adage until I came to London really, its origins stem from the Industrial Revolution in Britain. I grew up in non-European countries where these big industrial revolutions didn't take place, although its consequences could still be felt and seen, so perhaps that is why I didn't learn to divide my day like that. Personally, a big part of being an artist implies constantly questioning a lot of unseen structures, whether they are politically, socially or biologically driven. Where these structures stem from, why they are in place, who they benefit, etc. I've gradually come around to the idea that in my particular case, the idea of work, a workplace and working hours is a myth. The nature of my work implies changing environments regularly whilst I am researching or developing a piece. From doing field work, to going to labs, interviewing scientists or experts, or learning about their machinery or techniques. These tend to be extremely interesting spaces so in a lot of ways, although the switching off doesn't happen, these are my spaces of play too.

> What has changed about the balance between your working and waking life (in relation to light, clock-time, or always-on digital technology)?

Six years ago, I lived in a sunnier and warmer country and my routine was completely different to my current one. I think this was partly because of the cultural impact sunlight can have in understanding our daily rhythms. Even on a subconscious level, sunlight sends specific cues of the passage of time to our body clocks'. So when these cues don't take place, like in environments with artificial light, I think it is vital to find other strategies or signals that may help.

> What are you paying attention to (at the expense of your work or sleep)?

Brexit, the rise of far-right groups, the normalisation of fascist discourses, climate change, etc. And equally, trying to practice acts of care to those around me, and myself, to counteract their rhetoric of hate.

> What does art have to do with this (or, what do you want your artistic practice to communicate about life/technology/time today and in the future)?

In my work, I explore life through materials that are inert, static or ephemeral. Tracing through their complex histories, thinking about their connections with human ones, and exposing the manifold of relations that they hold. Each project

time and real space – a space in which the need for common good, in the form of sleep, is so blatantly self-evident, and space in which the most pathetically withered notions of ownership and capitalism are brandished like weapons to the detriment of everyone in the space – and nobody speaks up. And for what it's worth, everyone wants to be at least slightly well-rested when they arrive at their Parisian Airbnb to learn that it has iffy wifi and no towels.

Unavoidable sleep disruption is linked to the pie-slicing of our planet into twenty-four one-hour slices, and what happens when you mess with those slices. I may live in Vancouver, almost all of my business life involves time zones around the world. Vancouver lies on North America's west coast, the same time zone as LA. And in recent years, I've been getting those oddly annoying online meeting reminder messages which are being relentlessly bandied about in the Cloud:

> Hi... Tara here! Conference call Friday at 2:30 p.m. PDT. Craig and Shelley will be joining us from Palo Alto and they promise to have their PowerPoint act more together than they did last time LOL! And please, a reminder, all phones on airplane mode.

This is followed by the computerised tag:

> June 14 2:30 EST – 3:30 EST
> FRI-MCG-4-Seetharama Ramanujan (7)
> NYC-111-16-midtown 30f (6) [GVC]
> Meetingsys.cloud.com/MCG/NYC30f
>
> Tara@cloud.com
> Sara@cloud.com

IN YOUR DREAMS

Craig@cloud.com
Nikki@cloud.com
Trevor@cloud.com

is usually the result of long-term thinking, months of researching, allowing information to sediment and experimenting. I think recognising, acknowledging and respecting this goes against a lot of what 24/7 culture, and capitalism as a whole, is.

When these automated messages began arriving around 2014, I often found myself either one hour late, or one hour early for scheduled calls, and I'd then get a snippy email from a call organiser, always named Tara, reproaching me for my callous disregard for everybody else's time.

Teleconference meetings: let us not forget that they are suffocatingly dull, soul-crushingly pointless time-sucks that vaporise countless hours of people's time that would be better spent doing just about anything else. So, for me to receive a snippy memo from Tara is icing on mouldy cake. After a few rounds of this, I began investigating why this glitch kept happening, and what I discovered was this: Tara would input a scheduled meeting time, say 3:00, adding PDT (Pacific Daylight Time) at the end of it. Why would Tara add this? Easy: it's because writing '3:00 PDT' feels much sexier than simply writing '3:00'. (It really is, the same way ordering your drugs in kilos rather than pounds also feels far sexier.) But the thing is, there's not just PDT, but also PST (Pacific Standard Time) and depending on your time zone, you may or may not be in or out of PDT or PST, and if you put in the wrong one, I will be an hour early or late for your scheduled teleconference.

We inhabit the temporal ruins of an agrarian economy long made obsolescent, in which productivity can be tweaked by changing the nature of time itself. Twice yearly, newspapers run articles on why Daylight Savings is stupid etcetera, and how we ought to change it, but we never do. Oh, to live with Santa Claus or on the South Pole! Magic places where the time is always, and only ever can be, 0:00 o'clock.

I grew up in an alpine suburb of Vancouver so remote as to be technically rural, and until one gets their driver's licence at sixteen, one is effectively a prisoner of Nowhere. Fortunately, there was just enough bus service to get me down to sea level and into my first wage jobs at the age of fourteen: bussing tables at Ricky's Pancake House, then dishwashing at Pat's Spirited Fine Dining, then pumping gas at the Chevron at the Exit 7 offramp. I love work and would almost always prefer to be doing something rather than nothing. But at fourteen I discovered wage slavery: that I could trade hours for money, and this was a revelation: X-number of hours @ $4.25 per hour = new beige cord jeans and a shag perm.

It was only at the age of eighteen when this equation turned sinister. It was in the summer of 1980, when I was eligible to work on the massive Daimler-Benz assembly facility located in the furthest most reach of Stuttgart, Germany. Myself and nine other Canadian students were bunkered in what seemed like the only Bauhaus-inspired worker housing that had somehow avoided being bombed in WWII, and life there was like living in a Kleenex box along with thousands of other Daimler-Benz workers (from all across Turkey, Yugoslavia, Albania and the heel of the boot of Italy). Most of them, like me, spoke no German. In fact, I don't think I met three people in the whole place who spoke German.

Here's the thing: I was crazy stoked to be working there: Kraftwerk! Man-Machine! Metropolis! It was going to be posthuman. I would change my name to Florian, I'd get a cool German nose, and all of my emotions would conveniently vanish. It was also an astonishing hourly wage, I think it was $28.00 USD per hour, which was amazing then, and amazing now. But what I quickly learned is that assembly line

INSOMNIA IS BAD FOR BUSINESS

Douglas Coupland, *Slogans for the 21st Century,* 2011–ongoing

MONETIZING SLEEP IS DIFFERENT FROM MONETIZING DREAMS

Douglas Coupland, *Slogans for the 21st Century,* 2011–ongoing

work is numbingly repetitive; never glamorise it. You want to be as far away from an assembly line as possible. Time stretches on in the most fiendishly slow manner possible, culminating at that magic moment around Hour Six, when the clock actually starts ticking backwards. I remember the workers there dealt with the perversely slow passage of time by lubricating the working day with mini-bottles of Jägermeister from the snack trollies, starting during the first hour of work. So, if you own an early 1980s Mercedes Benz, take comfort in knowing that it was made by non-German-speaking Gästarbeiters riding seven-hour buzzes.

But here's the larger point: the Daimler-Benz job was swing-shift, which is great if you have the early Friday shift and don't have to be back until the late Monday shift – essentially a three-day weekend. But it's bad if your shift skews the other way: you have a Friday late shift plus the early Monday shift, so you get terrible sleep time and a crap weekend. This swing-shift is where I first felt personally conflicted about the industrial time-for-labour relationship: it wants to colonise your sleep, not just your waking time. This was disturbing to me... that someone, or a *thing*, could annex my sleeping life, and do so in a manner that left no room for rebuttal or flexibility. In mid-August I couldn't do it any longer, so I bleached my hair and moved to Munich for the remainder of the month. I began art school on Tuesday, 2 September, 1980.

I sometimes wonder if the reason we all go to school until our late teens isn't so much to gain knowledge or for society to keep kids off the street – rather, it's a way of enculturating future adults into the entirely artificial nine-to-five work week. There's nothing natural about the work week. It was arbitrarily made-up by human beings and mostly it... it just kind of stuck, and we don't ever question why we keep it. I don't know where the eight-hour sleep

29

number came from – I'm sure the Industrial Revolution was involved there somewhere. But now, with the neural complexities of the information era being grafted onto the industrial minds of the 20th century, I do wonder if sleep, our last remaining bastion of organic experience, is somehow in peril.

This essay is for a show called *24/7*, which is a funny coincidence for me, and let me explain. It begins with me saying that Americans are largely convinced Canadians are mostly socialists, and because of this most eBay vendors will no longer ship to Canada. This has forced me to rent a mail box in the tiny town of Sumas, Washington, a one-hour drive south east from my house along the Trans-Canada Highway. Sumas is like a town from a Stephen King novel: most of its businesses are shuttered up. There are no pedestrians. It once used to support a grocery store and some businesses but now it supports mailbox rental places like the one I use, called '24/7.' There's another mailbox place across the street called 'Ship Happens,' which is kind of funny, and I would have gotten a box there, had I seen it first. For over a year I've been going to Sumas every two weeks and my drive there has always been a happy driving ritual, enhanced by my playlist which is currently three-weeks and seven-hours long... (how long is yours?). The stuff I pick up in Sumas is mostly things I need for art projects, and most of it I buy online between about 22:00 and midnight which, a friend recently informed me, is the time window when men over the age of fifty make all of their big ticket online purchases, so it was a bit humbling for me to realise I'm the most banal kind of shopping statistic. And one need also remember that wait times at the border can be from one minute up to several hours, so it's kind of a form of temporal roulette to cross the border, even with wait times mentioned on the local AM radio traffic reports every ten minutes. For example, the US can reduce the number of crossing guards from five to one – or a heightened security alert can slow down interrogation time by a factor of three to five. And something seems to have happened in the past two months, and it's not just summer tourism... the Americans are simply taking much longer to admit people into their country, it's a fact. I don't like that a new wrench has been thrown into my shopping reality, the physical embodiment of our new asynchronic world of 24/7 online shopping, international borders and regressive politics. On the Canadian side of the border land sells for millions of dollars per acre and there's Starbucks; in Sumas there's silence and you can see silhouetted faces looking out at you from rooms that aren't lit from within. The overall sensation for me, is that of somehow shopping while I'm asleep. Did J.G. Ballard write a novel about this? He must have... because it's somehow becoming a real thing.

I was an early adapter to the internet at the beginning of the 1990s, so my brain got rewired by it a bit earlier than most others, but now we're collectively all in the same neural space.

I'm never bored yet I miss being bored.

If I forget my phone, my brain feels amputated.

In 1999 when I felt my brain changing, I put forth the notion that our brains were rewiring, and was dumped on from all sides. These days we all just take it for granted. We've reached a collective tipping point. What was once twenty-four pie slices around the planet has become billions of pie slices around the planet, and they're no longer in sequence.

Slogans for the 21st Century, 2011–ongoing (*I Miss Time* for Somerset House, 2019)

IN YOUR DREAMS

They happen whenever and wherever they want to and it is royally screwing with our heads... . We know our brains are fried. Time is shortening. Our lives will soon be over before we even realised they existed. Daylight savings, jet-lag, swing shifts, and the 21st century's endless dopamine hits – what's your own recipe for filling all hours of the day? Zopiclone? Ambien? Number of steps you took? Netflix? Likes and all that stuff? I think I'm doing okay, but then I look through a year's worth of iPhone photography and technically it looks like I did shitloads of things last year, but for me, inside my head, it all happened in a flash. Time didn't pass. It did, but it didn't. You know exactly what I mean. We're all strapped inside this ride together. I like it but I hate it, and I know I could never go back to the way things were before. I'm generally an optimist, but with regards to this, I think we're all slightly fucked. But mostly at the end of all of this, the thing is this: *I miss time*.

August 2019, Vancouver, Canada

Artist and novelist. Since 1991 Douglas Coupland has written thirteen novels published in most languages. He has written and performed for England's Royal Shakespeare Company and is a columnist for *The Financial Times* of London. He is a contributor to *The New York Times*, *e-flux*, *DIS* and *Vice*.

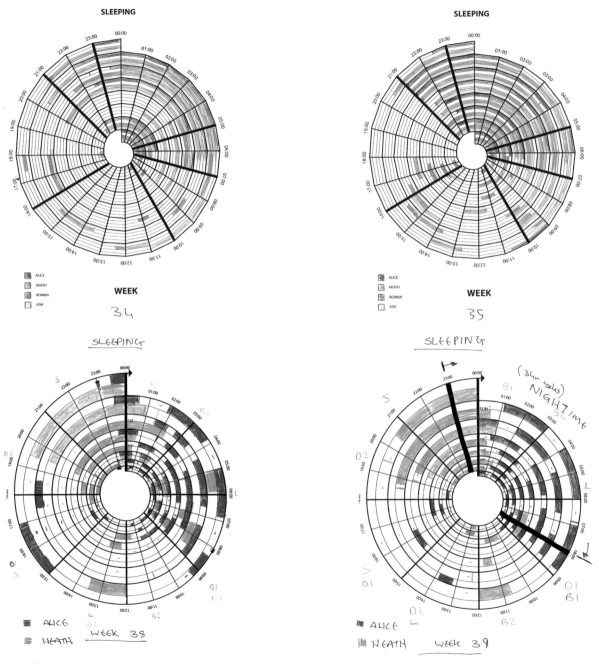

Heath Bunting, *Twin Charts*, 2015–2017

SLEEPING

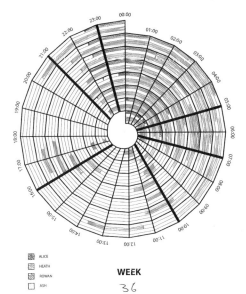

ALICE
HEATH
ROWAN
ASH

WEEK
36

~~FEEDING~~ / SLEEPING

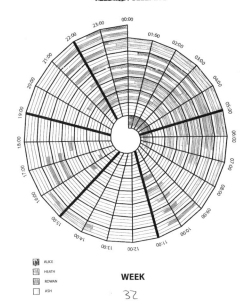

ALICE
HEATH
ROWAN
ASH

WEEK
32

SLEEPING

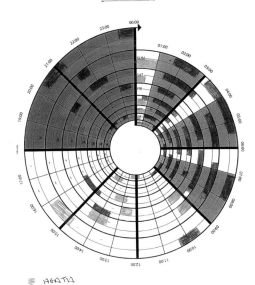

HEATH
ALICE

WEEK 40

SLEEPING

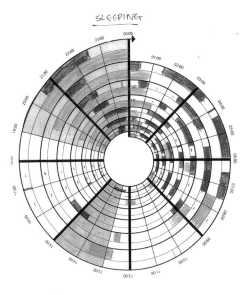

ALICE
HEATH

WEEK 41

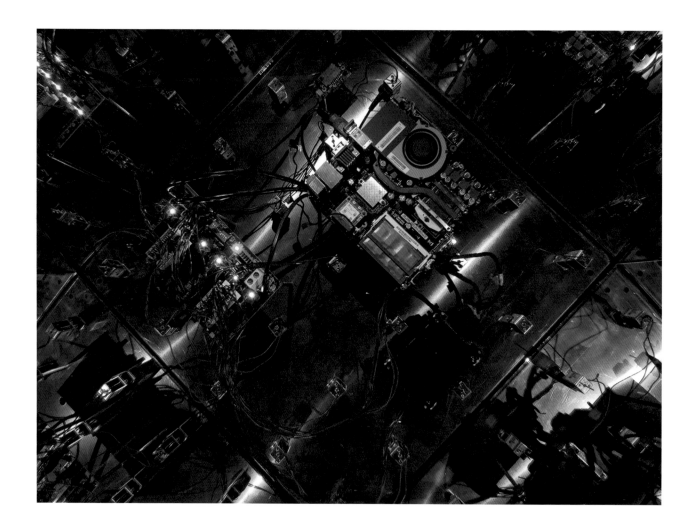

NONE Collective, *J3RR1. A Planned Torture*, 2017

THE WRECKAGE OF THE DAY

Dominic Smith

24/7 denotes the wreckage of the day as much as it concerns the extinguishing of darkness and obscurity.
—Jonathan Crary, *24/7: Late Capitalism and the Ends of Sleep*

'There's an app for that': *Sleep Better, SleepBot, Alarm Clock Xtreme, SnoreLab, Sleep Time.*

Take your pick.

There's a whole pile of books too: *Why We Sleep: The New Science of Dreams; The Sleep Revolution: Transforming Your Life, One Night at A Time; Why We Dream: The Transformative Power of Our Nightly Journey; Sleep Smarter: 21 Essential Strategies to Sleep Your Way to a Better Body, Better Health, and Bigger Success.*

There are deluxe and bespoke pillows and mattresses, therapies, massagers, diffusers, lights, candles, oils, and white noise machines. There's a whole litany of 'life hacks'.

And then there's the more pathological and pharmaceutical side of things: 'up to one third of Britons are suffering from insomnia at any one time', and, in the UK, 'around a tenth of people aged 16 and over take sleeping tablets three or more times a week'.[1]

Globally, the sleep aid industry, incorporating all of this and more, reached $76 billion in 2019.[2]

Is it possible to capitalise too much on sleep, or simply to know too much about it? What kind of strange paradox are we trapped in when all this industry and worry surrounds it? To what extent is your presence in this gallery or your attention to this catalogue part of all this?

It's all junk!
—Sarah Williams in *Labyrinth*

There is a memorable scene in the 1986 film *Labyrinth*. Jennifer Connelly's character, Sarah, trapped in the land of the Goblin King, is led by a witch through a junkyard to a replica of her bedroom back home. Sarah falls asleep on the bed. Waking, she utters the predictable line: *'it was just a dream'*. Getting up to explore, she opens a door.

1. J. Gabe, S.J. Williams and C.M. Coveney, 'Prescription Hypnotics in the News: A Study of UK Audiences', *Social Science & Medicine*, Vol.174, (2017) p.43–52, available, www.sciencedirect.com/science/article/pii/S0277953616306487
2. Darian Leader, 'Why the Sleep Industry is Keeping us Awake at Night', (March, 2019) www.theguardian.com/books/2019/mar/09/the-big-sleep-business-are-we-being-sold-an-impossible-dream

Reencountering the witch, Sarah discovers she is still in the junkyard. The scene becomes headily uncanny: the witch enters the room and desperately tries to convince Sarah she is at home. She does it by reminding Sarah of her material possessions: 'Oh your little bunny rabbit, you like your bunny rabbit, don't you [...] here are your panda slippers, you know how much you like your panda slippers!' the witch whines at her. Sarah resists. Sitting at her mirror, she starts to read her journal. Coming to the realisation that she still has to save her brother Toby from the Goblin King, Sarah exclaims: *'it's all junk!'* The walls come down. Sarah is situated fully in the junkyard, her bedroom obliterated.

I spent many an anxious night worrying about this scene as a child. Sometimes, having stolen through to my parents' room, I did this in their company. Judging by the comments on YouTube – where I recently re-watched the scene, bleary-eyed in the middle of the night – I am not the only child of the 1980s to have felt this way.

But there is an aspect of the scene I had overlooked: Sarah is not merely thrown back into the junkyard, she is thrown into a relation with her brother. At the beginning of *Labyrinth*, Sarah chafed bitterly against the duty of babysitting her brother, imposed on her by her parents. When the walls come down, her attitude has changed. It might look like Sarah is going to be a martyr or a heroine. She is, after all, eschewing the comforts of illusion and consciously going back for more punishment in the land of the Goblin King; and she is doing it alone, the very paradigm of a heroic individual. But in fact, Sarah goes after Toby not because she is required to, or because she is related to him, or because she wants to be a heroine. She does it because they are both in the junkyard, and she has recognised their shared condition of vulnerability. Her quest doesn't have her own fame or material wealth as its goal (yet more 'junk').

ARTIST INTERVIEW

Alan Warburton

Artist working critically with CGI software, hardware and virtual realities.

What is your relationship to 24/7 culture (as evidenced by the ceaselessness of contemporary capitalism)?

I work with 3D animation and visual effects software, a diverse and revolutionary set of 21st century creative tools that have accelerated our ability to create spectacular photorealistic imagery for television, film and commercials. These tools have automated tasks that would have been impossible just 15 or 20 years ago, yet as the tools get faster, more connected and more powerful, the artists must keep up – optimising their own labour to the standards of the machine, working ceaselessly for the benefit of the studios; studios that regularly hoard billions in profit. The CGI industry, despite its hypermodernity, demonstrates acutely the precarity of labour in human-machine collaboration: state subsidies, wage-fixing, forced overtime, burnout, outsourcing and sudden layoffs are normal in visual effects industry. They are the symptoms of the acceleration technology brings to work, and the collateral it demands.

How do you work/sleep/play (keeping in the mind the old adage of '8 hours of work, 8 hours of rest, 8 hours of what we will')?

I have always protected my sleep, for a long time it's been my only sovereign space. I can't imagine how others sleep so easily on trains, planes, on the floor of a house party or at work. Sleep for me is a space of isolation, control and calmness. I'd defend it with my life, but before I was at Somerset House I'd work at home, sleeping in the same room as my PC workstation. When I was rendering something for a deadline, I'd often work 20 hour days, sleeping, eating and working in the same tiny attic. As I drifted off, I'd dream of digital interfaces, and I'd never quite fall completely asleep, always tuned subconsciously to the whir of the computer fan, listening for the signs of a fatal crash, burnout from overclocking or the ever-present software bugs. I felt like a paranoid mother guarding a newborn, checking every 5 minutes to make sure my render was still going. The work I've made for *24/7* relates to this idea. Huge numbers of people all around the world are engaged in similar activity, babysitting complex computational processes to make sure they don't crash and burn. We're guardians of a new kind of incessant production, one with an inhuman kind of rhythm.

What has changed about the balance between your working and waking life (in relation to light, clock-time, or always-on digital technology)?

Around 2008, a divide emerged among my friends. Most of them upgraded to a smartphone, but the others steadfastly didn't. Texts would go unanswered, rumours would circulate that they'd moved to some remote village (some of them did) while the rest of us embarked on what seems like a new kind of symbiotic life, both cursed and blessed. We thrust ourselves into cities, worked harder and longer every year, all the time locked into painful contracts with our cherished devices. Sometimes we banish them in frustration or upgrade them as they grind to a halt. We cradle

THE WRECKAGE OF THE DAY

Sarah gets thrown into recognising conditions of solidarity where previously she had seen none.

This same move is made in Jonathan Crary's book *24/7*. Its retelling of our relationship to the junkyard that is late capitalism makes a delightful wreckage of a deeply engrained image of sleep as something 'private', 'individual', 'inward' or 'intimate'. In doing so, it highlights sleep as something collective, dependent, and with promising potential as a site of solidarity.

◌   ↻   ↺

Such acts of reimagination appear especially difficult today. This is because we are not merely living with an image of sleep as something 'private', restorative, and 'individual'. We are living with '24/7', Crary's term for an image of sleep that has, as an outgrowth of the 'private' and 'individual' image, become oppressive and exhausting for our times.

If the image of sleep as something fundamentally private and individual is what we might call the 'liberal picture', '24/7' is what might be called the 'neoliberal' or 'late capitalist' one. Whereas the liberal picture seeks to bank sleep as a kind of capital or possession, to be managed by the individual, the neoliberal one seeks to relentlessly mine, divide, spend and exhaust all that banked-up resource, in favour of norms of competition and efficiency.

For Crary, '24/7' is a 'state of permanent illumination' (p.5) and 'activity for its own sake' (p.15), an insomniac condition where 'we face the near impossibility of living humanely' (p.19), and a state 'shaped around individual goals of competitiveness, advancement, acquisitiveness, personal security, and personal comfort at the expense of

THE WRECKAGE OF THE DAY

others.' (p.41) This rhetoric might feel all too oppressive, the logic even nightmarish, but Crary makes it clear that this is exactly the point:

> [I]t might be objected that I have singled out exceptional or extreme phenomena, but if so, they are not disconnected from what have become normative trajectories and conditions elsewhere. One of those conditions can be characterised as a generalised inscription of human life into duration without breaks, defined by a principle of continuous function. [24/7] is a time that no longer passes, beyond clock time. (p.8)

'24/7' is not something to be empirically verified in terms of average experiences (a set of brain or body states, or an index of economic performance indicators, for instance); it is a kind of affective atmosphere we unconsciously inhabit, and that feels difficult to put our fingers upon in waking hours, but that lays an icy hand upon us in our more reflective and individuated night-time moments, however well-adjusted or average we might think we are.

If Crary's logic is nightmarish, it is because '24/7' is a nightmare.

The junkyard scene from *Labyrinth* was a nightmare for the mid-1980s. Reimagined for the nightmarish logic of '24/7', it would involve something like the complete luminescence of Sarah's room by military-grade spotlights.

Such artificiality is already at work in the scene in the way it is shot: the lighting, set and puppetry combine to land us in a kind of eerie 1980s twilight, where neither day nor night

them in anticipation of an awaited email or text or drop them in the rain at a bus stop and endure the months until we can upgrade and relieve our fingertips from the tiny microabrasions caused by swiping over smashed glass. I do wonder how those remote friends are doing, if they sleep better than I do. But they take months to answer their emails and they never told anyone their landline numbers.

> What does art have to do with this (or, what do you want your artistic practice to communicate about life/technology/time today and in the future)?

I'm always thinking about how the times we live through will be understood in retrospect, how we'll characterise the first quarter of the 21st century, especially the 2010s. My feeling is that we've lived through a kind of fragmented revolution: technology unified us, and broke us into a billion pieces at the same time. But it wasn't like one app or one piece of hardware did this, it was a rolling process of incremental change occurring at every level of society. Silicon Valley is turned onto this, it's still betting on the next big ripple of disruption from VR, machine learning or the blockchain. Disruption is the keyword for the 2010s, and it has inflected art too, not so much infrastructurally but conceptually. What is it to engage with technology when it's always changing? How can an artist make work that endures while also being timely, precise and integrated with tech? Can art survive the age of 'content'? Should it?

can be determined (a kind of 'Upside Down' from *Stranger Things*, *avant la lettre*, from the actual 1980s).

Reimagining the scene for '24/7' would involve dialling all of this up. But the scene would take on other dimensions as well. For one thing, the witch would disappear. Instead, the bewitchment would become more diffuse, atmospheric, and ambient. This is because '24/7' is a networked condition (really there, but starkly elsewhere as well – like so many Bitcoin servers or an enveloping 'Cloud'). Here, even the minimal requirements for finding solidarity with your enemies, such as shared space and time, have become moot and precarious.

Imagine being thrown into an online first-person shooter that you're not really invested in, and where you don't have much experience (the aesthetic and narrative of *Labyrinth* is, after all, very much like a videogame). You won't have had any time to build up rapport with anyone. Your enemies will be skilful, and will come at you from all directions. But they will also be dislocated from you, and you won't know who's a 'bot' and who's not. This gets closer to the sense of existential thrownness at stake in '24/7'.

Or, perhaps it's Sarah's possessions themselves that will come alive and start making demands of her in our reimagined version of the scene, as if linked to some hellish 'Internet of Things' or 'Everything Store'.

Even Sarah's journal will not be immune from this process. Sure, it will still be capable of saying reassuring things to her, and of acting as a portal to her brother. But it will also be networked in ways that link it to many other distracting things, and, before Sarah goes off to find her brother, it will nudge her to post something about it to her network... .

UBERMORGEN, *Chinese Coin (Red Blood)*, 2015

Julia Varela, *X/5.000*, 2016
Installation view: Exhibition *ARS17 – Hello World!* Museum of Contemporary Art Kiasma, Helsinki Finland,
March, 2017 – January, 2018

These images, like Crary's sketch of '24/7', are oppressive and exaggerated. But that's the point: they show how changed technological and historical conditions allow us to imagine different nightmares today.

↻　◌　↻

Frankly, I was hardly aware I even *had* a sense of sleep as something 'private' and 'individual' before reading *24/7*. On the other hand, I was well aware that I had a nightmarish image of sleep in today's world as something that is 'exhausted', 'divided', and 'spent' (not just for myself, but also for others). What my reading of Crary's book enabled was twofold: *recognition* of the first image as something longstanding in me, and a kind of *catharsis* of the second image.

When, in the throes of those *Labyrinth*-induced anxieties, I sought comfort from my parents, the image of sleep as something private and individual was somewhere in the background. It was the voice in the back of my head that said, 'Eventually you will have to walk down that corridor to your bedroom, and fall asleep alone'. When I looked up the junkyard scene on YouTube, there it was again, maintaining 'Isn't this a bit of an obsessive detour? Shouldn't you really be asleep?' And it was also in the background when I watched *Labyrinth* as a kid. It was the voice that wanted the oblivion of sleep for Sarah, not the nightmare of waking up in the junkyard. It was the voice that said, right at the start of the scene: 'Just stay asleep Sarah, don't get up!'

Reading *24/7* enabled recognition of these voices, and the book's journey through the logic of a nightmare allowed for a kind of reckoning with them.

But perhaps that all sounds a bit gloomy. If so, it's worth emphasising a third takeaway from Crary's book that ultimately emerges as much more important: *not what it has to say about nightmares, but what it has to say about different kinds of dreams... .*

It is easier to imagine the end of the world than it is to imagine the end of capitalism. That slogan captures precisely what I mean by 'capitalist realism'.
—Mark Fisher, *Capitalist Realism*

It is possible that [...] the imaginings of a future without capitalism begin as dreams of sleep.
—Jonathan Crary, *24/7*

How might sleep itself be reimagined as something akin to Sarah's realisation ('it's all junk!')?

The first thing to recognise is that Sarah's statement is both a realisation and an exclamation that has an effect: it describes her real state of affairs (in the junkyard), but it is also a speech act that makes something happen (the walls come down). There is a radical ambiguity here between passivity and activity: Sarah is both more stuck (in the junkyard) and more powerful than she initially thought (armed with small acts that can bring down walls).

Consider the two quotes above in this light. One opens Mark Fisher's 2009 book *Capitalist Realism*. The other closes Crary's *24/7*. As a term, 'Capitalist realism' captures what makes the nightmarish logic of '24/7' possible; it sums up a predicament of radical passivity (parallel to the predicament faced by Sarah): nowadays, when we are told to 'get real' or 'be realistic', the presupposition is that some form of capitalist cost/benefit analysis will ultimately provide the 'bottom line', and this leaves us more stuck than we initially thought, because it seems that 'there is no alternative' (unless, of course, we want to end up on some kind of 'scrap heap'...). In the junkyard scene from *Labyrinth*, it is the witch that reinforces this dearth of imagination in her commitment to the consolations of consumerism: 'Look, here are your panda slippers, you know how much you like your panda slippers [...] Everything you've ever cared about in the world is all right here... '.

By contrast, Crary's book identifies radical forms of activity that lie dormant across our apparently small and isolated acts of sleep.

In Fisher's account, 'it is easier to imagine the end of the world' not merely because our conditions of radical passivity are set by capitalism, but because capitalism easily capitalises on a view of imagination as a hardworking, productive, and fantastic form of 'activity'.[3]

In Crary's book, 'it is possible that [...] the imaginings of a future without capitalism begin as dreams of sleep'.

Here, *imagination*, *dreams* and *sleep* are themselves being reimagined as forms of radical activity akin to Sarah's

---

3. This is why it is not merely easier to imagine the end of the world under conditions set by capitalist realism, but also a potentially very profitable form of activity to do so (think of the generalised catastrophism of everything from clickbait and the news cycle, to zombie survivalist fantasy series, to an apparently endless reel of violent disaster and superhero films...). On radical passivity (think of the algorithmic logic of YouTube clips automatically playing one after another, discouraging you from turning the computer off and going to sleep), see Robert Pfaller, *Interpassivity: The Aesthetics of Delegated Enjoyment* (Edinburgh: Edinburgh University Press, 2017).

speech act (*'it's all junk!'*). Indeed, they are being reimagined as potentially *more* radical, because they provide a background against which acts like Sarah's can take place.

Whereas Sarah's statement is an extraordinary and one-off phrase that breaks a spell, imagining, dreaming and sleeping are, in Crary's account, recognised for what they always have been, and can be once more, once the spell of capitalist realism is broken: aspects of our everyday that are ambiguously active and passive (something we do, and that happens to us); that are held in common to be explored by all of us; that require the vigilance and care of others who are implicitly entrusted with watching over our shared world; and that provide alternative possibilities for futures that resist the profit motive.

Often, these radical activities course through us in silence. But they also have the capacity to roar.

In Fisher's account, it is so difficult to imagine the end of capitalism because we are complicit in capitalist realism and its picture of imagination. In Crary's account, to dream of sleep is what opens the space for imaginings which we do not seek to capitalise upon, and that do not remove us from our real conditions of existence (not all dreaming is 'escape'). Where two books like these are allowed to bookend one another, what is required to counteract the nightmarish logic of '24/7' becomes clear: a solidarity that has the courage to speak its mind in the way that Sarah does, backed up, not by capitalist realism, but by radical new forms of surrealism and new interpretations of dreams.

Let's not write this off as so much idealism. Let's call it dreaming, and let's celebrate the wreckage it might make of *24/7's* image of how our days are to be spent – like so many walls coming down through apparently small but accumulating acts... .

July 2019, Dundee, Scotland

Dominic Smith is Senior Lecturer in Philosophy at the University of Dundee and author of *Exceptional Technologies: A Continental Philosophy of Technology* (London & New York: Bloomsbury, 2018).

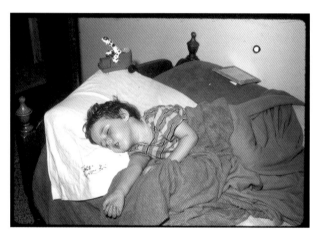

Adam Chodzko, *Sleepers. Hole*, 2012 [6, 10, 11, 12, 18, 29, 33 & 35]
Punctured found 35 mm slides, printed as C-types

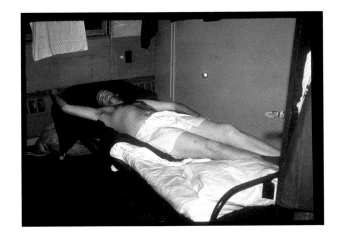

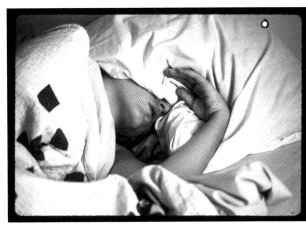

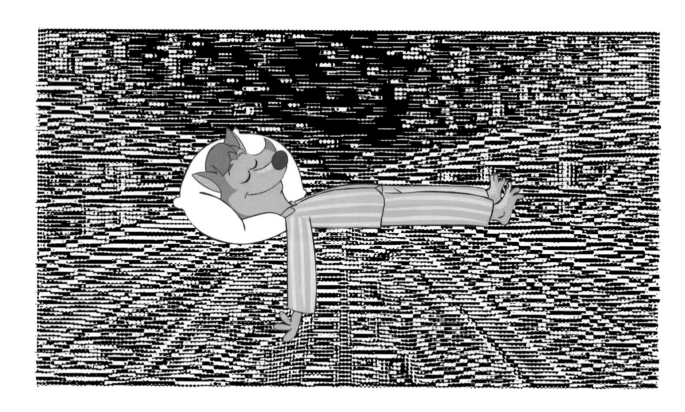

Ed Fornieles, *Sleeping*, 2015
HD Video, mp4, 3:00 mins

HOW TO SLEEP (EXTRACT)

Matthew Fuller

I DON'T WANT TO BE AWAKE

Poets turn the wreckage of love into verse; insomniacs turn the ruin of sleep into emails, lists, late-night radio, carpal tunnel syndrome, the circularity of nervous arguments, stupid intransigent loops of lost thinking. Alongside defecation, insomnia is one of the primary aspects of human culture that is universally enacted despite oneself. Disregarding those customs that should only be imagined on the basis of such a condition, insomnia is the culmination of our failures and convolutions in love, reproduction, work and money, that is to say that it is their inverse achievement, a photogram.

Insomnia is often characterised as resulting from circular thoughts; solipsisms become circuits. Thoughts shuttle back and forth in overwound snagging weaves: anachronistic memos of preemptive administration, things permanently undone and to be done. Thoughts that make their own claustrophobic maze: betrayals of love; the humiliation of

53

being left for another; the annoyance of not being able to think about anything else with any persistence or resolution in such a situation; inadequacy to the actions that are obvious if one takes cultural norms as a guide by which to act but which one cannot trust in any case and for wont of which one anticipates failing in the hopes of others and thus then has to offer some explanandum which must correlate in some way with one's own sense, which is not itself worth the candle in any case, being so obviously flawed given the present predicament. Strings of words that lose their object; the cretinising remembering of things that need to be done if the work is to succeed, the others are not to be let down, the children are to grow up well; disgust at oneself for becoming subject to such grinding notions as what is *well* but too lagged in fatigue to other than surrender to the circulation through such obscurities to engage in precise enough self-delusions to escape. These are delirium tremors of thought, but too bland for that, the twitching, the ticking, of daily stupidities, that when but written out seem simply like items on a list but in themselves are labyrinths with no feasible point of navigation but simply the exhausting compulsion to endure them. The soul tetchily emails itself with missing attachments and recalls of non-documents. It is so boring being so irritable, so productive of desperation – one that it seems might be resolved were one to fully wake up. But insomnia, with its insurmountable repetitions and knots, its circuitousness, its seeming endlessness is not absolutely distinct from normal waking states that simply colonise more areas of the sensorium with their repetitions, differing from them in part in that the chains of association and complication are, not less simply seen, but simply longer and more ramified in the quandaries they imply about why one is actually constituted by all this tedious quasi-individual thought stuff hanging together by a skein of normalities, customs, urges, hungers, habits, obligations, contracts, debts, mechanisms, prices and things. One feels as if it is one's own mind doing all this moronic braining, but surely they are there as a by-product of nerve tissues with only the inside of eyelids to gawp at and admire, conjuring up something to torture themselves on? It is an important ruse to be able to blame it on the nervous substrate and not what emerges out of it, nor that which it connects to and joins in the ensemble of its composition.

Insomnia provides all these things with their infinite branching, the splitting of possibilities, but also their haunting worried doublings, how they are seen and interpreted, by oneself, who may be wrong, who is so inevitably, and by the other who examines what passes for one's ideas or actions, the extent of whose maliciousness is unknown and who may be a boss, child, lover, committee, data trail. Sleep is a merciful chance to escape the treadmill of your own subjectivity.

LAWS GOVERNING SLEEP

Sleep requires a place, if only a patch of open ground, and it is tied to the cycle of the day, making it measurable. The location of sleep over time presents itself as an easy means to link social control to location and the assembling of a labour force. In the *Grundrisse* Karl Marx recounts the work of Frederic Morton Eden, a follower of Adam Smith, who working from the basis of parish Poor Law records, traced the late eighteenth-century inflation in the cost of everyday goods and food and wrote the first *History of the Labouring Classes in England*.[1] Amidst the catalogues of penalties for runaway apprentices and of the violent compulsion to

1. An abridged version is published as Frederic Morton Eden, *The State of the Poor: A History of the Labouring Classes in England, with Parochial Reports*, ed. A.G.L. Rogers (London: George Routledge & Sons, 1928).

ARTIST INTERVIEW

Helga Schmid

Artist/designer exploring the multifaceted nature of time in public, cultural and academic contexts.

What is your relationship to 24/7 culture (as evidenced by the ceaselessness of contemporary capitalism)?

For the past eight years, I have been observing and studying our 24/7 society, investigating today's time crisis. In reaction to this, I have developed the concept of 'Uchronia', a platform for critical and imaginative thought on the contemporary time crisis. It challenges our current perceptions, and offers alternative ways of being in time. I open up a new world of temporality (lived time) situated at the intersection of design, sociology and chronobiology. I use methods of unlearning, experimentation and systems thinking. By looking at the politics of time, especially contemporary work patterns and time norms, I propose an alternative approach on time and timing. I actively practice the implementation of designing time in workshops, experiential events and exhibitions. Uchronia advocates for temporal freedom and social change, promoting a positive relationship with and experience of time in the now, and the long now.

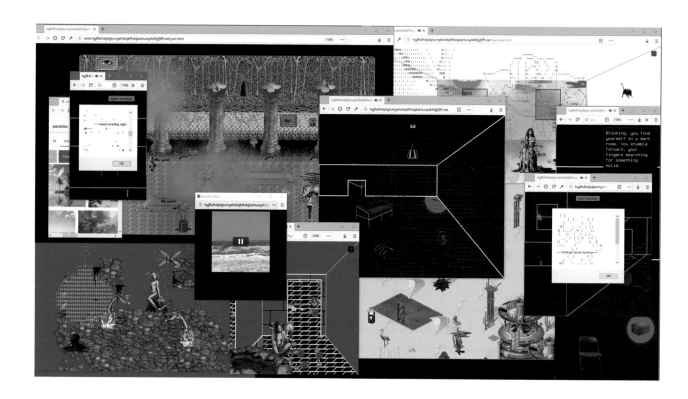

Cassie McQuater, *Black Room*, 2017

HOW TO SLEEP

work of the unemployed freed from villeinage but unable or unwilling to take work, he lists the degree to which sleep was regulated under the King, Henry VII.[2] Marx sees the regulation of wages in these passages as a boundary to the absolute 'subsumption' of life in capital. What however does that imply for the regulation of sleep, the explicit recognition of sleep and the customary need for a siesta, as a kind of counterpower to the full extension of the working day?

Mario Tronti diagrams the refusal of work, of exploitation, as prior to the possibility of explicit political theory: before politics gains a voice and a capacity to organise, there is rebellion.[3] Discipline in turn is a by-product of the problem of 'fixing' manpower, of making it predictable in behaviours and roughly reliable in quality. Sleep as a substance, as a state of matter, is certainly not inherently rebellious in this context, as it can be disciplined by the clock, bells, drugs and by other means, and is woven into the cycles of reproduction of the self, configured as working flesh, but it provides something both customary and biological, both idiosyncratic to the individual and the moment and part of species being, a conjunction of nature-culture, in Donna Haraway's formulation[4], that both pushes back against disciplinary forms of life and provides them with their matter, a necessity to organise, refine and productive of the self. If not productive, then locatable, fixed and available will suffice.

2. Karl Marx, *Grundrisse*, trans. Martin Nicolaus (London: Penguin, 2012), p.736.
3. Mario Tronti, *Strategy of Refusal*, (1965), available, www.libcom.org/library/strategy-refusal-mario-tronti/
4. Donna Haraway, *When Species Meet* (Minneapolis: University of Minnesota Press, 2008). The term 'nature-culture' does have the problem that it potentially implies the uniting of two previously distinct categories rather than formulating a term that notes the operation of that distinction where germane, but moves beyond its partiality.

How do you work/sleep/play (keeping in the mind the old adage of '8 hours of work, 8 hours of rest, 8 hours of what we will')?

My days are rather loosely structured in relation to seven bodily phases. I wake up naturally, without using an alarm clock. After a certain waking-up phase, a transition stage, I work quietly. In this phase, I try to disconnect myself, aiming for an undisturbed time of concentration. After this peak time, I eat, take a nap and rest for a while. Later on, I go outside, do some physical activity, rather than sitting inside. Followed by this, I return to my creative work, being mentally in a good, intuitive mindset. I work then up until I become sleepy. This is a moment in time for unstructured thoughts and ideas. Slowly, this transitions into sleep. Of course, this is an ideal day and the length of each of the phases varies hugely, depending on time of the year, my exposure to light and of the everyday work load. This structure is high up on my priority list and I make it happen as often as I can. But it needs a collective effort to implement other rhythms, then, I wouldn't need to fight for it so much as an individual.

What has changed about the balance between your working and waking life (in relation to light, clock-time, or always-on digital technology)?

I'm an early type, wherefore I never was forced to use an alarm clock to fit into the societal norm. But I realised the changes of the influence of light on my body, when I moved from the countryside (my parent's farm) to New York and later on to London. The impact of natural, daily rhythms and changing seasons diminished, and my life mainly happened indoors. It's now a very conscious act to bring natural day light into my everyday life. As part of my work, I look into alternative time systems and reject clocks as much as possible.

What are you paying attention to (at the expense of your work or sleep)?

My work is so entangled with the topic that I value sleep highly. I focus on a bodily related daily rhythm, and don't make such great divisions between week days and weekends or holidays. I rather look for a balanced daily rhythm, instead of working like a maniac towards the next bank or summer holidays.

What does art have to do with this (or, what do you want your artistic practice to communicate about life/technology/time today and in the future)?

Sleep and light have such a huge impact on the way we think and work. I'm often worried, that we limit our individual and collective creativity by not sleeping enough or not leaving space of exceptions to reflect or to contemplate. For instance, the chance, that a meeting right after lunch leads to something brilliant is rare and rather an exception. Many of us are in such a low point in concentration at this point in time that I don't understand why we collectively force ourselves through this. I see the potential in art and design to break out of the existing structures, and experiment with other rhythms of work and play. No device and no one else can solve or make these decisions for us. It's time to think more radically about our relationship to time. In the here and now, every day bears anew the potential to explore and experience Uchronia. Art and design can lead us in this new direction.

HOW TO SLEEP

A single night has so many bodies in it, so many sleepers with their intestines, eyeballs, teeth, limbs in various states of tonus or slackened musculature, tongues lying in mouths making their bed among teeth, so many parts moving in and out of sleep, so many sleepers who continue into the day, pass through the day. The continent of sleep that passes round the globe in darkness has routes cut through it by light, electricity and the demands of work.

As recounted in *Capital*'s section on the working day, nineteenth-century bakers turned up to work at night and mixed the dough in tubs for the following day's bread.[5] No loafers, they slept on boards over the dough as it proved, perhaps providing a little ambient warmth for the yeast, and woke two hours later to start working it, kneading and then shaping different kinds of bread. Here the length and place of sleep is determined by the actions and needs of a micro-organism within the dough. The hours of sleep are uncounted for by the wage but required by the work. There is a coupling between sleep that goes unfulfilled, and the liveliness of a minute entity, like raising babies rather than making dough. Yes, this is not a simple dual relationship but one scaffolded by conditions of work. Sleep occupies a seam of time that is to be mined by the employer, its satisfactory exploitation leaving the baker, at that time, with an average life expectancy of forty-two.

5. Karl Marx, *Capital: A Critique of Political Economy, Vol.1,* trans. B. Fowkes and D. Fernbach (London: Penguin, (1867) 1990) p.359–360.

HOW TO SLEEP

TRAINS AND BUSES

Sleep is a loss of alertness, a culturally understood passivity where the material of the body reneges on its requirement to produce a soul or active agency. Standing guard, watching out from the fire at the centre of the group or with an ear to the barricade, or waiting for the drone, the missile proudly named after the least useful member of the hive, is left to others, the young who like to patrol the perimeter. Turns are taken to sleep.

Sleeping on guard duty is a military crime, however. One's organs and limbs must be present and correct and ready for action, to watch, to shout warning, to alarm, to fire. The brain is in a purely supporting role, allocating and ordering the action of other organs and limbs in relation to the protocol of difference and engagement adopted. How many soldiers owe their lives to the dissimilarity between the knees of humans and horses, whose ability to lock into place while standing allows them their ability to stand and nap? Gravity is the heavy blanket that pulls the jointed body down to the level of the surface it lies on.

SLEEP UPRIGHT IN ORDER TO AVOID DEATH

Going further even than the body-experimenter René Descartes in his appetite to distinguish the mind from its mere vehicle, in the film *I Robot* (2004), (drawing on the novels by Arthur C. Clarke), sleep is something that a robot cannot do. People sleep, dogs sleep, but not machines. This is part of their torment and of their superiority, and the film's theme, how to escape from one's hard-coded imperatives, by luck, force of will, or through the contradictory interaction of rules and contexts, provides an analogue to the refusal of sleep. Sleep finds itself posed

Alice Vandeleur-Boorer, *Jet Slag: Around the world in 7 sleeps*, 2010

as a problem too in early plans for artificial intelligence. In Warren McCulloch and Walter Pitts' famous argument that the structure of the nervous system, including the brain, is formally equivalent to a dynamic network of logical propositions, the idea that an organism can emerge from sleep (as from anaesthesia, convulsions or coma) and maintain what it has learned is of some interest to them.[6] Why does one recur after a period in which the brain devolves to a lower level of activity? The gradual lighting up of a network out of lower-level stirrings is the soup out of which a consciousness evolves: the procedural opposite of the manager of the Café Mably in Jean-Paul Sartre's *Nausea* (1938) whose head, when the café empties of customers, making him lonely, becomes void and he sleeps.[7]

GO TO THE GUILDHALL MUSEUM AND LOOK AT THE CLOCKS.

There is something great, even democratic for all the falsity of that word, about the waves of night and of sleep running through the globe. Sleep is a planetary phenomenon, articulated variously in different species, a great quietening of breaths and, for some species, a chance to operate. For Gottfried Wilhelm Leibniz, thinker of the great flows and entanglements of being in *Monadology*, sleep as a lesser mode of consciousness or apperception, is, like

6. Warren McCulloch and Walter Pitts, 'A Logical Calculus of Nervous Activity', in Margaret Boden, ed., *The Philosophy of Artificial Intelligence* (Oxford: Oxford University Press, 1990) p.24.
7. Jean-Paul Sartre, *Nausea,* trans. Lloyd Alexander (New York: New Directions, (1938), 2013) p.8.
8. Gottfried Wilhelm Leibniz, 'Principles of Nature and Graces, Based on Reason', in *Philosophical Texts*, trans. Richard Francks and R.S. Woolhouse (Oxford: Oxford University Press, 1998) p.260.

them, something 'not given to all souls, and is not given to particular souls all the time,'[8] a grounds in turn for the belief among his predecessors in rationalist thought that sleep is a form of death. Consciousness pulses through the regions of the earth, synchronised to light. The planet, in its state of rolling light, becomes a space of an unconscious multitude throbbing with the vitality and variousness of its kinds. This rhythm is reciprocated in counterpoint in certain sectors of the globe with long throbs of gridded electricity for lighting, means of avoiding sleep, kerosene lamps, candles and fires. The latter is to keep what is awake away from those who are sleeping, the flames of the candles and lamps drawing moths to them as an imagined sun, one that is too close to navigate by.

© Matthew Fuller, *How to Sleep: The Art, Biology and Culture of Unconsciousness* (London & New York: Bloomsbury Academic, an imprint of Bloomsbury Publishing Plc., 2018).

Matthew Fuller is Professor of Cultural Studies, Goldsmiths, University of London.

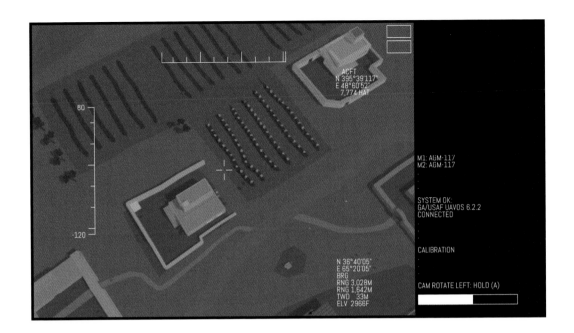

Biome Collective and Joseph DeLappe, *Killbox*, 2015–2016

Roman Signer, *BETT*, *5. Dezember 1996*, 1996
Pilot: Armin Caspari, Video: Aleksandra Signer, 4:15 mins

Rut Blees Luxemburg, *Enges Bretterhaus / Narrow Stage*, 1998
C-type on Aluminium, 150 × 180 cm

LIFE AND LABOUR ACROSS NOCTURNAL LONDON (EXTRACT)

Sukhdev Sandhu

THE PANOPTIC SUBLIME: AVIAN POLICE

Out on the edges of metroland in Loughton, Essex, along the traditional escape route for East Enders bolting from tuberculoid tenements to roomier suburban homes, lies a strange and little-known place called Lippitts Hill Camp. Black cab drivers get lost looking for it. When they do, it is hard for them to call for help: the thick foliage of nearby Epping Forest causes mobile-phone signals to splutter and die.

The Camp is recessive by nature. It shrinks from publicity. But it has a history to snag the imagination of all those with a taste for the subterranean and covert. During World War II, and right up until 1948, it was home to hundreds of Germans and Italian prisoners of war. A statue inside its iron gates marks their stay: 'Cut out of concrete by Rudi Weber 540177 while POW at this camp October 1946'. Later, the Royal Artillery Anti-Aircraft Operations were based here. Underground bunkers and gun pits are still visible.

These days, Lippitts Hill is used as a base by the Metropolitan Police Air Support Unit. Its officers are conquistadors of the London night. Each evening two crack teams of men and women set off from here and fly by helicopter across the capital. They're edge chasers, hurtling towards those spaces where ground officers fear – or are taught to fear – to tread: rooftops, railway lines, river banks. Their 500k machines, brimming with state-of-the-art hardware, allow them to scan the sprawling city, navigate it at great pace and elevation, and tail anyone who tries to carry out crimes under cover of darkness.

These avian police see, not just a side, but the entire face, of London. The rest of us, victims of gravity, stranded down on the ground, have to make do with squinting from the windows of easyJet planes or going for an evening ride on the London Eye. They do a job many of us can only dream of doing. Many of them, when they started out as beat bobbies, dreamed of taking to the skies too. Sometimes, after they had just been gobbed at by junkie pimps they were trying to arrest in Camden, or as they stood on Horse Guards Parade in full tunic and helmet with the midday sun turning the backs of their necks scarlet, they would hear the distant roar of overhead helicopters and think how nice it would be to be winched up.

The avian police see themselves as regular officers; before they begin their 7–7 shifts they sit around in the barracks watching European Championship football on Sky or reading authorised biographies of Ronnie Barker. But they are a select bunch: out of 30,000 Police Constables in the Metropolitan Police, only eighteen of them work in this Unit. As soon as the first call comes in, they leap into action, transformed by circumstances and technology into helmet- and harness-sporting redeemers of the night's blackness.

They become Supermen. Their helicopters give them exceptional powers. They can zoom all the way across the congested city in less than ten minutes. High-power lenses and thermal imagers allow them to make out the crocodile logo on a clubber's T-shirt from 2000 feet in the air, read number plates in the dark, look through the windows of Canary Wharf and spot canoodling office workers from eight miles away.

They can fly within fifty feet of Big Ben and cause global repercussions by shutting down Heathrow Airport. They can light up the ground beneath them by shining 30-million-candlepower 'nitesun' torches, and help to rescue suicidal young people or befuddled old people who have got lost in Hampstead Heath. Amateur crooks who have caught the odd episode of *The World's Greatest Police Chases* and think they know the principles of heat imaging hide under trees rather than, as used to happen, lying flat on fields: still they get detected.

> 'What's the most beautiful thing you've seen at night?' 'Oh, where do you begin? The mist lying in the valleys takes your breath away. The orange glow of the breaking dawn. Or sometimes when there's a full moon you can see its reflection in the Thames...'

The streets of London are made of gold. But only at night time and only from the sky. They lie there, glimmering like a Hatton Garden window display. Jewelled necklaces winking at us. At Piccadilly Circus and along Oxford Street the refracted neon gives them a ruby-red and emerald-green lustre. 'Cracking night, Sukhdev', pipes the pilot, but I am too awestruck by the city's beauty to reply. This is the panoptic sublime.

The helicopter flies in orbit. It waggles and tilts. At times

ARTIST INTERVIEW

Hyphen-Labs

Hyphen-Labs is an award winning, international team of women using technology, art, science, and futurism to test the boundaries of physical and digital space.

☾

What is your relationship to 24/7 culture (as evidenced by the ceaselessness of contemporary capitalism)?

Hyphen-Labs is an intercontinental entity born out of a need for 24/7 infrastructure. Our ability to exist and collaborate across time zones and landscapes benefits our practice, but it also means that the work never stops.

How do you work/sleep/play (keeping in the mind the old adage of '8 hours of work, 8 hours of rest, 8 hours of what we will')?

The work never stops, we inject sleep and play into our lives whenever we can. Our average arrangement is work 11 hours; sleep 7 hours; play 4 hours. The hours are flexible and change depending on the project, but art, and thus, our work, is intertwined between our waking and dreaming minds.

z^z^Z

The work never stops, we inject sleep and play into our lives whenever we can. Our average

LIFE AND LABOUR ACROSS NOCTURNAL LONDON

arrangement is work 3 hours; sleep 4 hours; play 17 hours. The hours are flexible and change depending on the project, but art, and thus, our work, is intertwined between our waking and dreaming minds.

z^z^Z

The work never stops, we inject sleep and play into our lives whenever we can. Our average arrangement is work 8 hours; sleep 8 hours; play 8 hours. The hours are flexible and change depending on the project, but art, and thus, our work, is intertwined between our waking and dreaming minds.

z^z^Z

The work never stops, we inject sleep and play into our lives whenever we can. Our average arrangement is work 1 hour; sleep 3 hours; play 20 hours. The hours are flexible and change depending on the project, but art, and thus, our work, is intertwined between our waking and dreaming minds.

z^z^Z

What has changed about the balance between your working and waking life (in relation to light, clock-time, or always-on digital technology)?

Notifications. Endless notifications.

What are you paying attention to (at the expense of your work or sleep)?

Dramatisations of reality. The noise on digital platforms. Using devices: hardware and software as a way to disconnect, circumventing the reality of being alone. How long will it take us to understand that we are actually human batteries just 'paying' attention with our time and 'likes' and that our digital worlds are accumulating infinite amounts of digital detritus?

it feels as if the pilot has lost control, an outdoor tightrope walker about to fall to earth. The stomach nausea is accompanied by bursts of landmark glee: there in the distance, is Wembley Stadium with cranes and machines perched over it like basketball players primed to slamdunk; there the Fabergé rugby ball of the Swiss Re Tower.

Politicians and demographers often assert that London is overloaded, crammed to the hilt, but from the sky it appears far from congested. The concrete jungle is nowhere to be seen. Even the most built-up areas are punctuated by large expanses of dark forest, empty parts of the city's night canvas. The capital is an endless origami unfolding, stretching out horizontally rather than vertically. Its residential buildings are so crabbed and timid that any that stick out appear both heroic and lonely.

The sky is constantly lit up as private planes carrying Russian billionaires to vital soccer fixtures start their descent, and a whole queue of commercial airliners begin stacking to come into Heathrow; the effect is that of a corporate quasar game as lights continually strafe the darkness. Things invisible at ground level suddenly rear into view: industrial parks – there seem to be hundreds of them. And while, even from Primrose Hill or Greenwich Park, the city melds into one largely unindividuated flatscape, at night time it becomes more composite in character, a loose and disconnected set of Lego pieces. One pilot describes Croydon as 'an oasis of high-rise buildings, sitting there like downtown Dallas'.

'Do I like night time?'
'Of course. When I was a bobby I used to go to the top of this tower block that had Big Ben in one direction and Thames Bridge in the other. At 3.30am, 22 floors up, you could hear it strike: for that few minutes London was quiet and you could hear the birds singing.'

70

Pierre Huyghe, *The Housing Projects*, 2001

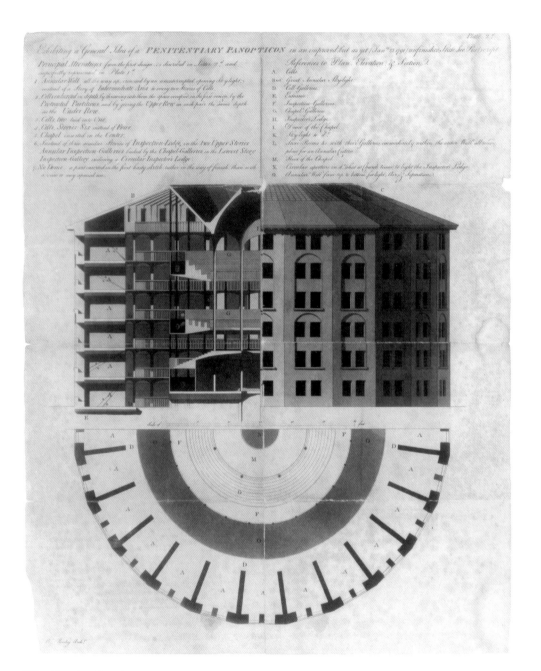

Willey Reveley, *Drawing, after Bentham's design, for the Panopticon or Inspection House – a new type of prison*, 1791
Drawing, section and plan of the building, *Bentham Papers* 115/44

LIFE AND LABOUR ACROSS NOCTURNAL LONDON

The avian police, like black cab drivers, rely on The Knowledge. Spatial awareness is crucial. They cannot afford to be disorientated, even though they may have had to spin around a trouble spot half a dozen times and at different speeds and altitudes. New moving-map systems allow the back-seat navigator to type any address or postcode into a machine and, at the press of a button on the camera controller, have the camera pointing not just in the approximate vicinity of their destination, but at the precise house number or floor level.

It helps them to be as precise as homing pigeons. Yet, with single global positioning system (GPS) screens able to accommodate only a quarter of an *A–Z* page, and the threat of computer malfunction an ongoing possibility, few officers have thrown away their guide books. They carry customised cartographies, special versions of the *Collins Atlas* in which traditional features have been overlaid with police boundaries and London letter codes for all the police stations. They each supplement this information with biro'd squiggles of their own, creolising the official geographies with private mnemonics for particular parts of the city. The lights near Wormwood Scrubs resemble a dog bone.

Before the moving maps were introduced, pilots learned to navigate London by its dark areas. Well-known landmarks were often obscured by fog, so they were forced to become airborne sensualists, feeling out and alert to the shapes and contours of forests and verdant areas. Victoria Park, it was generally agreed, looked like a boot.

'What's it like in winter?'
'It can be like being inside one of those snow balls. The snow comes at you from every angle. White dots spitting at you. If you watch *Star Trek*, it's like going into warp drive with all the stars coming at you. You don't

What does art have to do with this (or, what do you want your artistic practice to communicate about life/technology/time today and in the future)?

'I want Wisdom, but Wisdom's only friend is time / Who I, I run away from / But he always catches me and walks faster than I ran' – Spooks.
Art takes time. But because of 24/7 culture... we can't catch it.

experience snow like that normally – travelling at that speed and horizontally.'

It is overcast tonight. The clouds we skim and fly through are disorientating. They make it seem as if smoke is rising, as if the city is ablaze. We hover briefly above a mist-obscured St Paul's Cathedral and for a moment I feel I have been transported back to World War II and the scene of that iconic photographic of Blitz London in which Christopher Wren's dome is surrounded by acres of bloodied devastation.

The helicopter's thermal-imaging cameras irradiate the city. It looks skeletal, postmortemed. On the screen, its nocturnal hues and tints are reduced to black and white heat traces. Bleached and decoloured, it has become furtive, like a Customs' X-ray of immigrants smuggling into the country in the back of a lorry. The cameras induce suspicion: why has that snake of light suddenly concealed itself? – actually, it is just a train that has entered a tunnel. Every moving vehicle, at least initially, appears to be a portable terror container, a nuisance bundle to be monitored and tracked.

The attack on the World Trade Center and now the suicide bombings in London have led to the avian police being placed on constant alert. Heli-routes that fly near key financial and political institutions are almost out of bounds. Each day the pilots are supplied with security updates which assess the threat from terrorists to 'prominent and representational interests' belonging to the USA and Israel. One pilot describes his colleagues below as 'ground troops'. The thermal imagers themselves, though they are designed to help the police protect the city, produce images that resemble Baghdad, Vietnam – bombing zones for Allied troops. For a moment, London's nocturnal beauty vanishes: the forests seem ash-charred, lit-up areas ghostly apparitions.

'What's the most beautiful thing I've seen? After a storm – when the city looks so washed and lovely. When it's a misty night, you can just make out the tops of high buildings like Canary Wharf: they look like islands in the mist...'.

The avian police have to listen to six radio channels at once, a non-stop, mid-air, cross-town traffic of police sirens, command centre requests, breaking news about pick-axe-wielding Turks on rooftops, random bursts of white noise. But they are also soundscape artists who bring noise to night London, calibrating it to create minimal or maximal impact. Too much roar gives suspects sound cover to break windows or climb fences. Too little, and would-be criminals think they can do as they please.

It would be an exaggeration to call the police sonic terrorists. But they do use sound as a weapon. On quiet nights without remand centre breakouts or high-speed motorway chases, they fly out to patrol London's crime hotspots in poorer boroughs such as Brent, Tower Hamlets and Southwark. When they see clumps of youths hanging around, they make the equivalent of a handbrake turn in the air. The blades cut the air harder. There is a loud thumping and chopping sound and everyone looks up to see the word 'police' on the underside of their machines. 'They've all watched *Air Wolf* and think we can see through walls', laughs one pilot, 'We're not going to tell them otherwise'.

'What do we see that no one else sees? You can see everyone's swimming pools. There's also some absolutely outstanding roof gardens down in the City. Certain areas like Chingford have a love of chequered patios. You've got a run on orange and cream tiles in Barking and East London at the moment: a B&Q lorry must have been turned over.'

75

Flying over a city, especially at night time, allows a brief glimpse of freedom. It is to be liberated from the stress and murk of terrestrial life. Towards the end of their shifts, as darkness slides almost imperceptibly towards dawn, the avian police start to fly back to Lippitts Hill Camp. Their heads ache and their backs are sore, but though they are at a low ebb physically, for a few minutes they relax a little and let their minds wander. They think of their families and of past loves. They look at the line of pollution that hangs above the city, so thick they could walk on it, and wish it could be disappeared. They look at the city twitching into motion below them and are touched by its fragility. How beautifully Hampstead rises out of the mist.

A pilot, his operational lingo replaced by dreamy reverie, reflects on his working life in London:

> 'When I was working on the ground I certainly didn't like the city. Quite the opposite. But everywhere's lovely from the air. Even the worst bits look good. Like King's Cross: I never noticed the architecture of St Pancras before – all the stations and the buildings are fantastic. To be honest, I'd rather spend more time in the air than on the ground. Whatever you see on the horizon you can go to. You feel like a giant because the world is smaller.'

Reprinted from Sukhdev Sandhu, *Night Haunts: A Journey Through the London Night* (London: Artangel and Verso, 2007) p.20–27. Reprinted with permission of the author and of Verso.

Sukhdev Sandhu was the Founding Director of the Center for Experimental Humanities and is an Associate Professor of English and Social and Cultural Analysis at New York University, and author of books including *London Calling: How Black and Asian Writers Imagined a City*, *I'll Get My Coat* and *Night Haunts: A Journey through the London Night*.

Unknown Maker (France), *Empire Type World Clock* (for indicating time around the globe), 1909

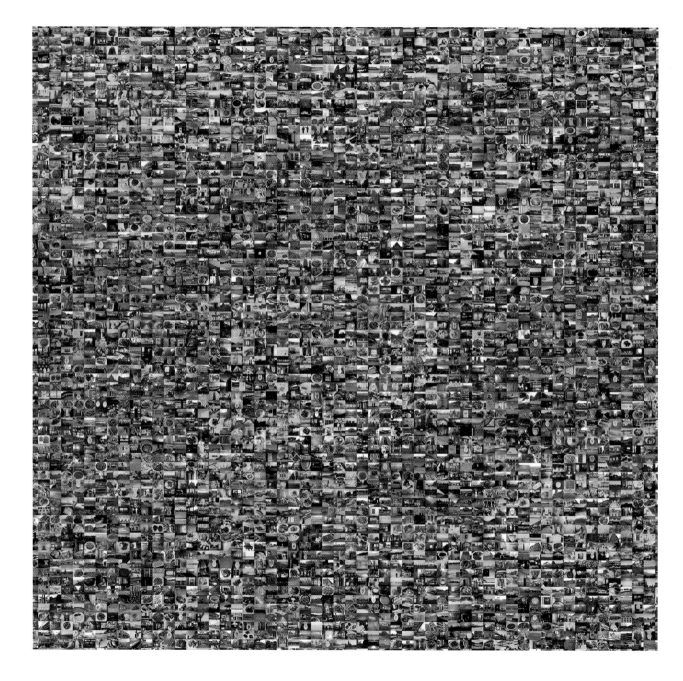

Hasan Elahi, *Scorpion W2* (detail), 2019

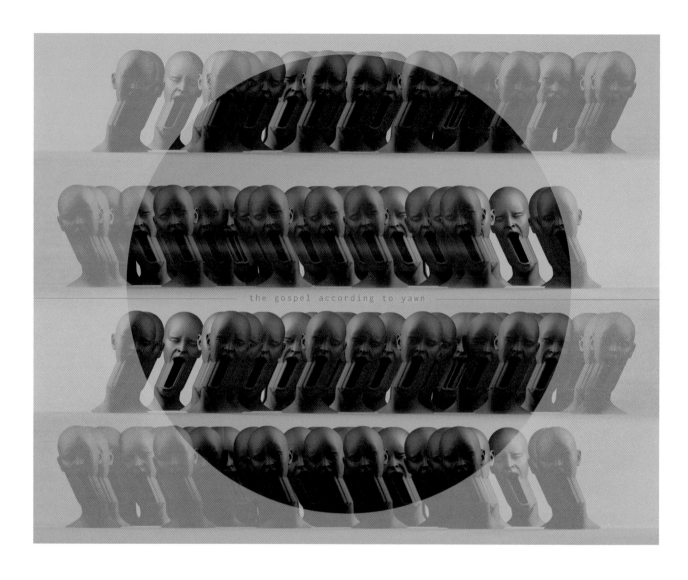

the gospel according to yawn

Hyphen-Labs, *The Gospel According to Yawn*, 2019

SPEED TRAPS AND THE TEMPORAL (EXTRACT)

Sarah Sharma

SPEED-UP AND ALL OF ITS TRAPPINGS

At the turn of the 21st century, a set of questions that focused on the impact of technologies built for acceleration and faster-moving capital on the democratic fate of a sped-up globe emerged across the disciplines. I refer to this line of critical inquiry as 'speed theory'. Paul Virilio was one of the first to write of speed in this vein, in 1970s France, and he remains its most prominent figure. But the critiques of the culture of speed continue to accelerate.[1] Speed culture goes by many epitaphs: 'the 24/7 world' (Hassan 2003; Crary 2013) 'liquid times' (Bauman 2000), 'hypermodern times' (Lipovetsky, 2005), 'the culture of acceleration' (Tomlinson, 2007), 'the coming of immediacy' (Tomlinson 2007), 'dromocratic society' (Armitage, 2000), 'the new temporalities of biopolitical production' (Hardt and Negri,

1. Paul Virilio, *Speed and Politics,* trans. Mark Polizzotti (New York: Semiotext(e), 1986).

81

2000), 'the chronoscopic society' (Hassan, 2003), and chronodystopia' (Armitage and Roberts, 2003).[2]

While critical theorists of speed examine different elements of speed culture, there is a shared sentiment:

2. Robert Hassan, *The Chronoscopic Society: Globalization, Time, and Knowledge in the Network Economy* (New York: Peter Lang, 2003); Jonathan Crary, *24/7: Late Capitalism and the Ends of Sleep* (New York; London: Verso, 2014); Zygmunt Bauman, *Liquid Modernity* (London: Blackwell, 2000); Giles Lipovetsky, *Hypermodern Times*, trans. Andrew Brown (Malden, MA: Polity, 2005); John Tomlinson, *The Culture of Speed: The Coming of Immediacy* (London: Sage, 2007); John Armitage, *Paul Virilio: From Modernism to Hypermodernism and Beyond* (London: Sage, 2000); Michael Hardt and Antonio Negri, *Empire* (Cambridge, MA: Harvard University Press, 2000) and John Armitage and Joanne Roberts, *Living with Cyberspace: Technology and Society in the 21st Century* (New York: Continuum, 2003).

Of course, the advent of the new millennium isn't the first time speed has been the object of critical inquiry. Such work fits within an important trajectory of thought that includes histories of capital as it became coterminous with different technologies and their temporal and spatial effects. Such critical histories describe clocks, trains, telegraphs, and other global metronomes with their attendant temporal dictates of ticks, tocks, nanoseconds, and light years (Karl Marx, *Capital: Volume 1,* trans. B. Fowkes and D. Fernbach (London: Penguin, (1867) 2002); E.P. Thompson, 'Time, Work, Discipline and Industrial Capitalism', *Past and Present,* Vol.38, (1967) p.56–97; Stephen Kern, *The Culture of Time and Space 1880–1918* (Cambridge, MA: Harvard University Press, 1983); Wolfgang Schivelbusch, *The Railway Journey: The Industrialization and Perception of Time and Space* (Berkeley: California University Press, 1987); James W. Carey, *Communication as Culture: Essays on Media and Society* (New York: Routledge, 1989); Moishe Postone, *Time, Labor, and Social Domination: A Reinterpretation of Marx's Critical Theory* (New York: Cambridge University Press, 1993); Jay Griffiths, *A Sideways Look at Time* (New York: Putnam, 1999); Peter Galison, *Einstein's Clocks, Poincare's Maps: Empires of Time* (New York: W. W. Norton and Company, 2003) and Paul Glennie & Nigel Thrift, *Shaping the Day: A History of Timekeeping in England and Wales, 1300–1800* (Oxford: Oxford University Press, 2009).

new technologies and faster moving capital herald grave political and social consequences. 'Speed' is the commanding by-product of a mutually reinforcing complex that includes global capital, real-time communication technologies, military technologies and scientific research on human bodies. Democratic deliberation gives over to instant communication, or what Virilio refers to as 'live contemplation'. Political interaction is replaced by monetary transaction. Space, the apparent *real* ground of politics, is subsumed by speed. 'Real-time is not very different from classical tyranny, because it tends to destroy the reflection of the citizen in favour of a reflex action'.[3] Speed theorists argue that geopolitics (a politics based in space) is supplanted by chronopolitics (a politics based in time). The yielding of space to time not only dissolves the grounding of politics but it gives rise to a way of being in time that is antithetical to the political public sphere. Speed theory is without a doubt indebted to Marx's formulation of the clock's quantification of work and the production of value and socially necessary time. Part of this analysis includes attention to the new social formations that arise because of accelerated capital and technologies including the changing quantity of labour time versus leisure time. They align with Marx's formulation of socially necessary time.[4] Speed theory is also largely sympathetic to E.P. Thompson's thesis in 'Time, Work, Discipline and Industrial Capitalism' (1967) concerned with how the new chronometers imposed by governmental, military, and capitalist interests have replaced earlier, collective perceptions of time that he believed flowed from the collective wisdom of human societies. Marx and Thompson are both necessary to thinking about how capital

3. *Speed and Politics,* op. cit., p.87.
4. *Capital: Volume 1*, op. cit.

ARTIST INTERVIEW

Tekja

Data visualisation studio producing data driven digital experiences which reveal the stories and patterns hidden in complex information.

What is your relationship to 24/7 culture (as evidenced by the ceaselessness of contemporary capitalism)?

Like most people who live in urban society, we take full advantage of the 24/7 lifestyle, we carry out our lives pretty safe in the knowledge that urgently needed items can be delivered to our door the next day – food can always be bought, long-distance communication is immediate and entertainment is at our fingertips, all of our needs can be met almost instantaneously. But this convenience sits in real tension with our knowledge about the impact of this 24/7 lifestyle – increased pollution, ruined habitats, depletion of natural resources and, on a more personal level, fundamental changes to our natural circadian rhythms resulting in people living 'out of sync' with natural daily cycles, a rise in prevalence of insomnia and sleep disorders, most disturbingly among children.

How do you work/sleep/play (keeping in the mind the old adage of '8 hours of work, 8 hours of rest, 8 hours of what we will')?

Like many young professionals in busy periods our work follows the weekday / weekend cycle, rather than a daily routine of rest, work and play. Instead we work solidly most weekdays, sleeping where we can. The weekend is for catching up.

Whilst in busy periods 24/7 life can be relentless, it can also complement a balanced and happy life. The shift from physical to digital interaction offers the ability to shift and split the working day to fit around family commitments and work and hobbies. It also means we can work with clients around the globe without needing to travel for hours to meet face to face.

What has changed about the balance between your working and waking life (in relation to light, clock-time, or always-on digital technology)?

Since forming our own studio, we don't watch the clock in terms of how much we work, we set a defined set of tasks and complete them each day. Sometimes we finish early, sometimes late but this ability to take charge of the daily routine offers a real sense of freedom from the repetitive grind of office hours that we have both previously experienced.

What are you paying attention to (at the expense of your work or sleep)?

The smart phone. It can become an extension of the self, almost always at arms reach it is the one thing that, whether bored; looking for distraction or hoping to relax, we reach for.

robs the worker of time, whether by diminishing personal time, controlling the bounds of a working day, stalling clocks, or establishing the age limits of child labour. Yet the protagonist in the theoretical critiques of speed is no longer the worker or any specific subjugated population for that matter. Instead, it is a generalised individual who feels suddenly out of time. The subject of value and the subject of most attention in the critique of speed is the same subject who confirms speed-up most readily as *the* new reality – whether the jetsetter, the financial worker, public man, or the theorist. While pointing out the indentured conditions of contemporary labour and living brought on by ubiquitous technologies is an important analysis of contemporary life, it does not deal with the uneven cultural politics of time. The theory of social difference that emerges out of speed theory revolves around a simplistic binary. Zygmunt Bauman, in *Globalization: The Human Consequences* (1998), maintains that 'the inhabitants of the first world live in a perpetual present, going through a succession of episodes hygienically insulated from their past as well as future. These people are constantly busy and perpetually short of time, since each moment in time is non-extensive'.[5] He goes on to say, as for the slow class:

People marooned in the opposite world are crushed under the burden of the abundant, redundant and useless time they have nothing to fill with. In their time nothing ever happens. They do not 'control time' – but neither are they controlled by it, unlike the clocking in, clocking out ancestors subject to the faceless rhythm of factory time.[6]

5. Zygmunt Bauman, *Globalization: The Human Consequences* (New York: Columbia University Press, 1998) p.88.
6. Ibid.

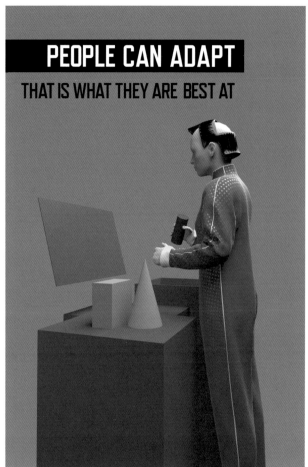

John Butler, *Xerox's Paradox*, 2018

John Butler, *Xerox's Paradox*, 2018

SPEED TRAPS AND THE TEMPORAL

In the end there are only two temporal poles of chronopolitical life that are dealt with: fast classes and slow classes (Virilio, 1986), tourists and vagabonds (Bauman, 1998), inhabitants of chronotopia and chronodystopia (Armitage and Roberts, 2003), and the time rich and the time poor (Rifkin, 1987).[7] These two temporal classes are imagined to be much like ships that never pass. And, neither seems to meet the temporal requirement of civic life; where one should be contemplative and deliberative as a form of political temporal composure.

Theories of liberal democracy assume a way of being in time, but the assumption itself is not a time politics; it is one single, and albeit very powerful, discursive mobilisation of time.[8] What continues to animate public sphere theorising is an expectation that political civic life is only political insofar as it *takes place in a space and time separate from state and market*. The right practice of time, a democratic one, must be free of institutional restraints, whether economic or cultural. It is a time that must be unfettered in order to be contemplative.

Speed theory espouses a conception of the public conditioned upon a politics of time that is about the *pace* of one's time rather than how its citizens or denizens are *constituted in* time. The democratic expectation, to be free

What does art have to do with this (or, what do you want your artistic practice to communicate about life/technology/time today and in the future)?

24/7 living has crept into our lives almost unnoticed with activity gradually encroaching further and further into the night.

We search for digital trails that reveal hidden patterns in the way we live. To reveal how far the 24/7 society has blurred the boundary between night and day. We are tapping into the voices of those searching for sleep. Revealing how far sleep has shifted from the natural hours of darkness around the world.

7. *Speed and Politics*, op. cit.; *Globalization: The Human Consequences*, op. cit; Jeremy Rifkin, *Time Wars: The Primary Conflict in Human History* (New York: Simon and Schuster, 1987); *Living with Cyberspace*, op. cit.
8. See for example William E. Scheuerman, *Liberal Democracy and the Social Acceleration of Time* (Baltimore and London: Johns Hopkins University Press, 2004).

and have time, is a liberal bourgeois demand that lends itself better to arguments for lifestyle choices like 'how do you do it all' rather than recognition of the politics of time.

The theoretical calls to *slow down* function in a very similar vein.[9] Within this slow-living imaginary, time is treated as something to which we all have equal access.[10] Slowness is not outside of the normalising temporal order. It encompasses its own particular ideological time claims and beholds its own exclusive temporal practices. There is a dominating sensibility within this discourse on slowness that being a 'good' political citizen requires transcendence. Transcendence pervades in both taking the necessary time out and abstracting oneself from the energy and traffic of everyday life. But this traffic conditions the very possibility for some to transcend. Slowness, as a form of managing or resisting speed, is in and of itself not a time politics. Slowing down does not necessarily change (and certainly does not ameliorate) the ways in which individuals and social groups are tangled together in time.

Speed-up as a descriptor of the moment is hard to shake. I suggest it is compelling for a few mutually reinforcing reasons: it justifies a culture of overwork and overconsumption and the unnecessary exhaustion that comes with it. Speed-up justifies the need for the labour of others to help maintain and reproduce the conditions and quality of one's own life, including one's exhaustion. But speed-up might be less an accurate description of the world than it is a universalising polemic promulgated by those threatened for the first time by the possibility of not being

9. See Wendy Parkins and Geoffrey Craig, *Slow Living* (Sydney: University of New South Wales University Press, 2006).
10. Sarah Sharma, *In the Meantime: Temporality and Cultural Politics* (Durham, NC: Duke University Press, 2014).

in control of time. One doesn't have to venture far to offer up the observation that theories of the world speeding up and out of control are written almost solely by men in the Western academy. But this is hardly an adequate intellectual conclusion on my part: to suggest that time is far more multiple and differential than this masculinist discourse of speed-up has assumed and leave it at that. I offer a cautionary tale regarding the discourse of speed and its circulatory power; it is not speed per se but the explanatory power of speed that is responsible for perpetuating inequalities at the level of time. The temporal is a corrective to the discourse of speed-up. I suggest the temporal complicates the narratives of speed-up that permeate culture and theory, but also that a temporal perspective into speed is necessary in order to account for how time is actually lived across the social.

ENTER THE TEMPORAL

Across the landscape of everyday life, interventions into time are presented as invitations to experience a novel temporal experience – to slow down, take a breather, nap, meditate, and rest at work on-site and on demand. We are witnessing the emergence of infrastructure of temporal care built around maintaining the time needs of particular subjects. By 'time needs' I mean the discursive construction of one's lifetime and time of life being of particular importance to the contemporary moment. Temporal architectures are composed of built environments, commodities and services, and technologies directed to the management and enhancement of a certain kind of subject's time – a privileged temporality. For someone like the contemporary business traveller an immersive environment oriented around their time maintenance combines technologies and human labour that allow them

ARTIST INTERVIEW

Iain Forsyth and Jane Pollard

Artists and filmmakers working across installation, performance, sound, film and TV drama.

What is your relationship to 24/7 culture (as evidenced by the ceaselessness of contemporary capitalism)?

Perhaps it's part of the human condition to feel we're living on the brink. The most ceaseless, thoroughly modern life. Maybe every age feels the whoosh of this unwitting rollercoaster. As the ride continues, our bodies, these fallible shells that house us, feel like they'll soon be incapable of taking the ride any more. The gap widens between what our minds can imagine and what our bodies are capable of. One day we'll step off, to let the next generations race past. For us, Bill Hicks said it best: 'the world is like a ride in an amusement park, and when you choose to go on it you think it's real because that's how powerful our minds are. And the ride goes up and down and round and round. It has thrills and chills and it's very loud and it's fun, for a while. Some people have been on the ride for a long time and they begin to question: "Is this real?" And other people come back to us and say, "Hey, don't worry, don't be afraid, ever, because this is just a ride." And we... kill those people.'

How do you work/sleep/play (keeping in the mind the old adage of '8 hours of work, 8 hours of rest, 8 hours of what we will')?

For twenty five years now we've built our world around our work. This is the only true way we understand ourselves, and the world around us. So too, our play is built around work. It's impossible to engage in one, without the potential of the other. This is *LIFE*, entwined and messy. Work can be playful, and work has the potential to present moments of play – social, open, shared, enjoyable encounters. This flows both ways. Sleep is something we fit in. That doesn't mean we don't love it. We embrace the ritual of giving yourself over to nothingness. To abandoning consciousness and attempting to repair and recharge the damage done to mind and body. Sleep is like the bottom of the ocean – it is largely unchartered terrain. There's so much there to learn, incredible secrets to be revealed. What lurks down there is conditioned to exist only in the dark. Sometimes we get lucky, and catch a glimpse as consciousness de-rails each night, or re-rails each morning. The trick is, to keep looking.

What has changed about the balance between your working and waking life (in relation to light, clock-time, or always-on digital technology)?

We've never succumbed to those regimes that regulate your body clock. Having kids, say, or working a 9–5 job. But we have fallen deep to the screen-filled culture of digital technology, communication and entertainment. Screens steal so much of our time, over and above that which is freely given. It's terrifying to see how hard companies work to keep you transfixed. TV has the next episode lined up before credits have rolled on the last. If you like this, you'll also like this. An endless void, dragging us to the bottom. Here's hoping that all these constant attempts to predict our behaviour will make us all try harder to think and behave unpredictably.

SPEED TRAPS AND THE TEMPORAL

to recalibrate and get resituated within the particular time demands of global capital.

Take for instance Minute Suites, appearing across American airports. These WIFI-powered napping suites replete with desks, beds, workstations, and a on-site service staff offer the paying airport guest the chance to recharge and work or nap in private.

The rise of a temporal architecture elevates the cultural significance of waiting from the dead time of doing nothing to a time of self-improvement and a privileged moment of reprieve. Everyone manages time in one way or the other, for better or for worse. But for most populations, the management of time is more or less private and invisible – hidden from the view of others. And even for subjects of value at the airport, for example, waiting has not always taken on such a public character. It was done in exclusive lounges with other temporally compatible subjects. Today, the emerging architecture of time maintenance designed for the business traveller offers a public display of busy-ness where they can retreat privately in public view. People exercising good time management are visible everywhere and culturally applauded for doing it so well. There they are managing their time like pros and making good use of the architecture of time maintenance erected for their labours. These technologies of time maintenance reinforce the idea that subjects of value cannot be easily replaced, but the secondary labour they depend upon can.

The speed theorist also reinforces this value when they focus solely on new technologies and a singular experience of time. If this business traveller and their Minute Suites and all the gadgets and productivity apps that adorn them

90

were generalisable across the social fabric then perhaps the argument could be made that this is a culture of speed and the politics of time needs to be directed toward dismantling this tempo. But the continued focus on this population and this tempo, in theory and in the consumer market, obscures attention away from the other temporalities that labour in order to maintain this time. One need not even have to look past the Minute Suite concierge to see the differential temporalities that compose the architecture of time maintenance. Thinking politically about time requires attention to these temporal entanglements and how time is experienced as a form of social difference.

One's relationship to the temporal order of things, the value of their time, can be rendered visible by how time is strategically managed and controlled. This is where the politics of time intersects with time control. The control of time is never individual; it is always collective. To achieve time control, to work toward it constantly, could be an empty political goal. The ultimate desire to control one's time is not a sufficient endpoint or starting point for politicising time.

'I CONTROL MY OWN TIME, I CONTROL MY OWN TIME, I CONTROL MY OWN TIME.'

Mohammed is a London Uber driver. He provides bottled water, crisps, and biscuits in the back of his Uber. He has a mini-vacuum he keeps in the front seat so he can quickly clean up the crumbs. It is Saturday in Central London around midnight. The pub patrons are home already and the clubbers still clubbing. Midnight is quiet in this part of London. The next rush is hours away. Mohammed tells me he had started a career in computer engineering but

What are you paying attention to (at the expense of your work or sleep)?

The heaviest price paid is always daydreaming. The opportunity for the mind to wander, to go somewhere that isn't screaming for your attention. There's always something, the ring, ping, alert, vibrate telling us there's something to look at, check up on, catch up with, keep on top of. Or something you've already missed. The right to be bored is worth fighting for. Only then can we open up the roads less travelled.

What does art have to do with this (or, what do you want your artistic practice to communicate about life/technology/time today and in the future)?

The responsibility of art, we believe, is to enable change. Art may not be able to change the world, but it can change people. And people can, and do, change the world. Art is a way of exploring new terrain, drawing the new maps. Before the developers move in to pave paradise and put up a parking lot.

after a year of uninspiring days working at a desk under a strict management team he felt like he was wasting time. Becoming an Uber driver felt like the 'ultimate freedom'. He tells me that he really enjoys the work because it lets him be in control of his time. He makes this proclamation right after relaying he has spent the last thirty minutes quite bored and waiting in his car for a fare. Mohammed doesn't really take entire days off either. He sometimes decides in the moment if he is going to drive or not. If he's out and feeling bored or not having fun or just sitting around at home and feels guilty about not working he turns his phone on. This sentiment echoes other workers in the gig economy made up of menial outsourced labour.

TaskRabbit is an online outsourcing company that helps busy people 'live smarter' by connecting them to people within the vicinity who can take care of a range of domestic errands like furniture assembly, grocery shopping, and cleaning. Their tagline reads: 'We'll do what you don't want to do, so you can do what you love.' The New York Times (August, 2014) recently ran an exposé on workers in the sharing economy at Fiverr, TaskRabbit, Uber, and Lyft.[11] One of the taskers profiled was a single mother who had spent almost sixteen hours doing menial work for others that included assembling Ikea furniture, gardening, and taking someone to the airport before the crack of dawn. At the end of the day she has worked well beyond an acceptable workday. She also has a backache and a tension headache to show for it, along with 200 dollars. She recognises that it was a good day in terms of cash but not a sustainable livelihood. She expresses that the ultimate pay-off for this

11. Natasha Singer, 'In the Sharing Economy, Workers Find Both Freedom and Uncertainty', The New York Times (August, 2014) available, www.nytimes.com/2014/08/17/technology/in-the-sharing-economy-workers-find-both-freedom-and-uncertainty.html

type of precarious work is that at least she can control her own time.

The invoking of time control in these two examples is set against another temporal condition of generalised precarity – the unguaranteed future. In fact, the mention of the control of time actually refers to a tiny slice of time: control over one's immediate working conditions, sometimes the hour, in the absence of security. Even if the boss is decentralised and diffuse, incarnate in every transaction, the relationship is fleeting and more palatable than other types of workplace domination and exploitation. Likewise, those who need task rabbits suggest that the technology 'greases an otherwise awkward exchange'.[12] Taskers and Uber drivers plug in and plug out when they want to. They determine the length of their working day as well as their own geography. As a type of labour that is downloaded on demand, they might not know the exact contours of their day or even what they will be doing the next hour but their labour gets to feel like a choice even if there is so clearly no choice but to work. Having control over one's time in the absence of security and with the promise of labouring under temporal parameters of the day one chooses seems like an acceptable trade-off.

Originally published in Judy Wajcman and Nigel Dodd (eds.), *The Sociology of Speed: Digital, Organizational, and Social Temporalities* (Oxford: Oxford University Press, 2016). Reproduced with permission of the author and the Licensor through PLSclear.

Sarah Sharma is Associate Professor and Director of the McLuhan Centre for Culture and Technology at the University of Toronto.

12. 'In the Sharing Economy, Workers Find Both Freedom and Uncertainty', op. cit.

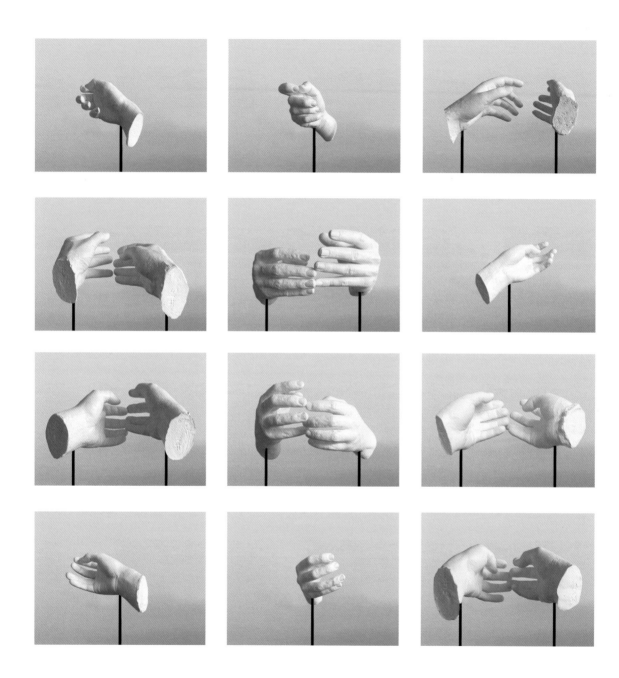

Esmeralda Kosmatopoulos, *Fifteen Pairs of Mouths*, 2016–2019

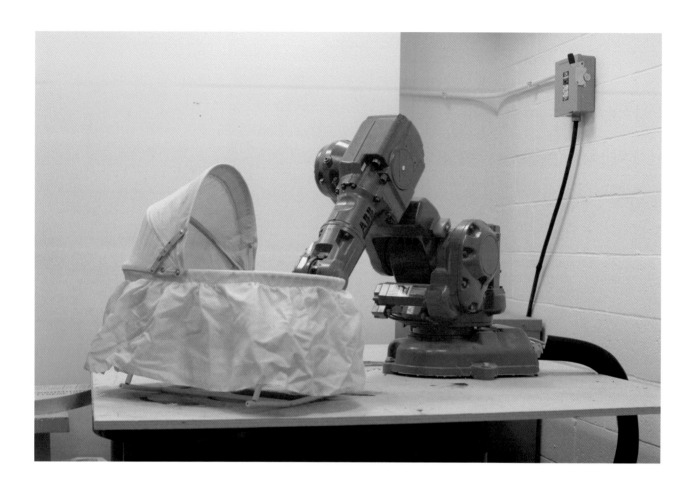

Addie Wagenknecht, *Optimization of Parenthood, Part 2*, 2012
ABB robotic arm, bassinet, custom software, dimensions variable

WORK IN THE AGE OF THE DEVICE

Esther Leslie

OUR OWN DEVICES

We have accommodated ourselves to devices. Devices need us, as much as we need them. Our bodies complete their circuits. We work for the machine in touching it. The touch that the touchscreens of our phones and tablets rely on makes of the body an instrument. Gestures that we make towards our devices, all day, most days, make connections – between us and the tiny events that are triggered on and through the screen. Connected to the device, we are divided into our own bubbles of social labour. Devices divvy up each of us into little packets of circumscribed screen-directed attention. In dividing us up, the device evokes an etymological connection. The word comes from the late thirteenth-century Old French, derived from the Latin '*divisus*', that which has been divided. When goods were being divided between people, a mark, known as a device, which took the form of an emblem, was put on each item to show whose was whose. A device is something that belongs to someone as an act of division. A device may also be literary, such as those devices a rhetorician or author might employ to gain best effect, or an advantage. Devices are things that separate, distribute and mark out.

But as much as we are divided, we partake of a language, one designed to be interpreted by the screens who read us. And so our gestures must be common enough to be read by the machine, even if the machine is our device, our own one. Our gestures are not ours. They belong to the machinery. At the start, just one finger demanded reactions from the screen. Now it is multi-touch and the screen reads a body, its pinches, whirls, flicks, sometimes its specific amount of pressure or pulse of successive taps. One jab and the screen starts up. Then it reacts to the fingertip, the knuckle, to the tap and swipe. The screen's surface is smooth and geared up to respond. In turn, the fingertips and other parts of the fingers become sensitised in new ways, developing gestures not executed hitherto, such as the thumb and two finger gesture of enlargement. The device's surface is a receptive sheet, or appears to be so. In actuality it is the top of a sandwich of functions. Liquid crystals' own lively gestures are channelled into simple flippings of switches: on/off.

The body's gestural repertoire changes in dialogue with the new machinery. Fingers communicate with the smoothness of the screen, a flatness that is a new geometry of active surface space, something like Walter Benjamin's *Spielraum*, a coinage that might be translated multiply as play space, room for manoeuvre, field for action or wiggle room.[1] New

1. See Walter Benjamin, 'The Work of Art in the Age of its Technological Reproducibility' (2nd version), in *The Work of Art in the Age of Its Technological Reproducibility and Other Writings on Media*, eds. Michael W. Jennings, Bridget Doherty & Thomas Levin, trans. Michael W. Jennings (Harvard University Press, Cambridge, MA, 2008) p.45.

technologies – from aeroplanes to cameras to matches – were directed to liberate humans from toil, spreading seed from the air, making images at the press of a button, lighting fire at the twitch of fingers. Scope for play is vastly extended. New technologies extend leisure time. New technologies also crack apart the world in new ways, making it into a space of experimentation, or play, providing new sights, novel experiences, in which human and machine interpenetrate. *Spielraum* is a realm of exploration, of active participation in the new geometries that are invented by technologically produced and distributed forms. In Benjamin's account, a new human is nascent in the era of industrial and technological capitalism. It is one who connects in altered ways with, in, and through the world, and is learning how to move around this new world. This body is adaptable to new experiences of space and time, recomposed through apparatuses and through images. The touch screen might, however, represent the limit point of *Spielraum*. Benjamin's positively valued concepts of distraction and tactile engagement – whereby things are grasped by the hand, met halfway, consumed as a matter of habit – are pushed into something more like permanent commotion of a massive, limitless outside and the limited touching point of compulsively prodding finger tips. A finger binds its bearer to a massive system. Touch screen technologies are annexed to networks, which allow for constant updating and a seemingly limitless accessibility across space. What might have been conceived as a space of play is appropriated in various ways as a space of work, even if this work acts as a kind of play.

Devices nowadays are presented as machineries of freedom. Devices sell mobility – the ability to roam, but never be out of touch, the ability to draw stuff down from the cloud and out of the fogged network of *things* and not be limited by physical location. The device offers the

99

ARTIST INTERVIEW

Ted Hunt

Independent speculative, critical and discursive designer.

What is your relationship to 24/7 culture (as evidenced by the ceaselessness of contemporary capitalism)?

I'm a conscientious objector.

How do you work/sleep/play (keeping in the mind the old adage of '8 hours of work, 8 hours of rest, 8 hours of what we will')?

I've become more and more seasonal in my work/sleep/leisure patterns – increasing productivity with the longer days of summer and decreasing it in line with the natural states of dormancy found in nature in winter. This is also reflected on a daily basis, where I'll begin to disengage with productive work at sunset, whether that's late afternoon in winter or late evening in summer. As an independent designer I've no set formula of how I divide each 24 hours up, I'm privileged in that what I do for work overlaps with what I do for leisure, so as long as I get enough sleep everything else sorts itself out pretty naturally. I've currently been looking into the chronobiology of nature and came across the phenomenon of 'diapause' as a period of suspended development, especially during unfavourable environmental conditions. Given the rate of overproduction and consumption that is driving the climate crisis I'm considering adopting it myself and potentially taking a long-term/short-term/seasonal hiatus in my practise as a means to negate the accelerationism that I contribute to by default. I read a quote by the economist Mariana Mazzucato recently, 'the way the word "value" is used in modern economics has made it easier for value-extracting activities to masquerade as value-creating activities.'[*] I think the same is true of what we call 'progress' and 'productivity' and that a lot of what we're accelerating ourselves into is doing far more harm than good. Deterioration masquerading as progress. So perhaps an active strategy might be to just take our foot off the accelerator now and again. And that draws us nicely back to the 24/7 argument that we need to reclaim the distinction between day and night, between the new normal of being 'always-on' and simply being off.

What has changed about the balance between your working and waking life (in relation to light, clock-time, or always-on digital technology)?

I've now realised that my previous formal working life was aligned with the clock and routines of the workplace as my entrainment cues (the external environmental cues that living organisms use as alignment signals for their body clocks). Now I've consciously tried to align my entrainment cues to natural phenomenon such as sunrises; sunsets; the dawn chorus; vegetation etc.

WORK IN THE AGE OF THE DEVICE

freedom to work where and when one wants. The device makes work always potentially accessible, in making the human resource always potentially accessible. The device figures at the heart of the contemporary Human Resource concepts of 'Enterprise Mobility' and 'BYOD' (Bring Your Own Device), as presented, for example, by Citrix, a 'mobile workspace' company:

Because in this new era, work is no longer a place – it's something you do anywhere inspiration strikes.[2]

The freedom of 'Bring Your Own Device' happily translates, the target of the online advertising is told, into company advantage, because 'device flexibility is key to employee productivity'.[3] For the employer, so the boosterish copy reveals, other benefits include cutting expenses, because fixed workplaces and infrastructure are unnecessary. Through the device, the whole labouring capacity of the worker is subsumed and made into resource, as illimitable labour power inside and outside of paid-for work situations. The device spills work everywhere. The device spills work – or the creation of value – into all of life. Work is a mode and a mood of being.

MOOD AND WORK

Monitoring emotions is now standard HR practice. Team Mood is an application that follows groups of workers at 'team' level, requesting that they input their mood at regular intervals.

Pilvi Takala, *The Stroker*, 2018

Pilvi Takala, *The Stroker*, 2018

WORK IN THE AGE OF THE DEVICE

At the end of the day, team members tell if they have the feeling of having a good or a bad day. These analytics are a tool for the team for continuous improvement.[4]

There is nothing but continuous improvement. The mood of the team can be infinitely improved, always on the up. This is an example of the quasi-Japanese management philosophy of *Kaizen*, the incremental and collective pursuit of improvement in organisation, materials, and workflow, derived from the Toyota Production System to eliminate wastage, of matter, time, labour power.[5] It is extended into emotions.

In the digital age, the practice of HR has been reinvigorated by the prospects of mining data sources relating to its human subjects, workers or potential workers. This granular analysis becomes a science of atmosphere, of corporate mood, of office ambience. Digital systems facilitate the accessing of data about the managed human resources in a number of ways. Workers are tracked and analysed using digital applications known as 'Software as a Service' designed for 'human capital management'. The digital programmes and procedures go by various names, such as Workforce Analytics, Human Capital Analytics or Talent Analytics. Those selling the packages, and with it, the ideology of talent analytics and other vogue phrases, claim to be leveraging data to create predictive analytics models for 'human capital'. That is to say, they promise to divine the future. Analytics inform employers, for example, who is likely to leave the organisation or who is working more productively, allowing strategies to be put in place to make efforts to hold onto those who are more

4. Team Mood, www.teammood.com/en/
5. Masaaki Imai, *Gemba Kaizen: A Commonsense, Low-Cost Approach to Management* (New York: Mcgraw Hill, 1997).

What are you paying attention to (at the expense of your work or sleep)?

Reflecting on being a circadian organism rather than just a Homo Sapien. Humans make up just 0.01 percent of living organisms in the biosphere, and yet we've become entirely insular and locked into that tiny fraction of reality. If you pick up a newspaper, pretty much everything in it will concern that 0.01 percent of reality. Nearly all of the remaining 99.99 percent of living organisms exhibit either a direct or indirect relationship to the sun. My thinking is that if we can increasingly see ourselves as circadian organisms we'll come to realise what it is like to be interdependent beings in a much wider biosphere. A part of nature, rather than apart from nature.

What does art have to do with this (or, what do you want your artistic practice to communicate about life/technology/time today and in the future)?

Art has traditionally articulated the unarticulated. The philosopher Federico Campagna, has said of my work, *Circa Solar*, that it, 'takes the familiar notion of "time" and transforms it poetically into a mysterious object, capable of hosting simultaneously darkness and light, poetry and technology, rebellion and mythopoiesis. The mark of any profound transformation of the world corresponds to a radical transformation of time: *Circa Solar* stands like an open gate on the path to the next cosmological revolution.' I'm trying to resurface our cosmological relationship to the Sun as the enduring and naturally apparent measurement of 'time' which predates the artifice of 'the time' represented by mechanical clocks.

'talented' and let go of those who are not. Analytics are a product of now available massive pools of data, which can be evaluated at various scales and granularities. 'Quantified workplaces' collect data concerning employee performance, productivity, number of keystrokes, turnover rates, employee retention, employee engagement and overall job satisfaction, and more, all of which is monitored and analysed automatically.[6] Workers may be requested to log their rates of stress, well-being, subjective sense of productivity, sometimes on a Likert scale of 1–5, conveyed through little pictograms of button faces which range from a large smile to a downturned mouth. A scale of 1 to 5: there may only be room, at least in the administered world, for five emotions. Each bit of data is a clue to future moves on the part of the floating 'specks of human capital'.[7] Such analytics might be able to track a general shift in morale or mood as it sweeps across a company. That emotions and mood are key indicators is evident in the rise of another digital analytics field, which is Emotion Analytics, or Sentiment Analysis. New techniques of emotion tracking through computers have been directed at workers – as well as consumers – in various ways. Beyond endless online surveys monitoring emotional states, microphones collect data on language and tones of voice in the workplace. Audio mining techniques and a correlation engine ascribe the labels of human emotions to those monitored words and tones.

The identification and logging of mood, or of attention, is a widespread capacity of machines, integrated, for example,

6. Daniel Enthoven, 'Quantified Self? How About A Quantified Workplace?' (2013) available, www.wired.com/insights/2013/05/quantified-self-how-about-a-quantified-workplace/

7. Wendy Brown, 'Neoliberalized Knowledge', *History of the Present*, Vol.1, No.1 (Summer, 2011) p.113–129, 127.

British Time Recorder Co. Ltd. (London, England), *Time Recording Device used at the Central Telegraph Office*, London, 1905

Étienne-Jules Marey, *Man Walking*, 1890–91

into digital cameras with their 'smile detection', open eye recognition, and face detection technology, a routine element of the newer Perceptual User Interfaces. A smile is not hard to characterise and a machine can easily learn how to recognise it. In detecting smiles, the software looks for open eyes and an upward curved mouth, once it identifies a face or faces on the screen. Some cameras allow users to differentiate between small smiles and big grins, so that the camera knows exactly what to look out for to achieve the desired shot. Of course, emotions have been created for machinic devices before. The history of photography involves the structuring of faces so that the machines can read them. Sometimes image makers invented further devices to ensure they extracted the requisite emotion. In 1862, Duchenne de Boulogne produced a text book, *The Mechanism of Human Facial Expression,* on the muscular basis of emotional states – at least the impression of such – with photographs and discussion of the use of electrical currents directed at certain muscles of the face – muscles of joy, muscles of sadness, of surprise and fright.[8] Body and emotions are hinged, naturally and also as a capacity that can be forced to produce. The machine's attention exacts specific emotions, by activating muscles that contort the face. These generated emotional states are likely not felt or experienced internally. The frame in which they are induced – electrical shocks, cold metal spikes and so on – would likely induce other emotional reactions. The text book is an early example of how it is possible – certainly in the age of the photograph or machinic stare – to make a database of emotions that will lend itself to becoming operative.[9] Emotional life can be produced and reproduced as image. Charles Darwin used

8. G.-B. Duchenne de Boulogne, *The Mechanism of Human Facial Expression* (Cambridge: Cambridge University Press, (1862) 2006).
9. Zoe Beloff, *Emotions Go To Work* (Colchester: Minor Compositions, 2018) p.18.

some of the images in his 1872 volume *The Expression of the Emotions in Man and Animals*. The shock-inducing apparatus had been erased in the reproductions for print. These muscular contractions become evidence of felt states. Duchenne's stimulation of muscles to produce certain faces is a grotesque version of the way in which the machine schools its subjects in facial presentation. The role of the photographic subjects is to produce out of themselves a controlled image, which they have been trained to regard as appropriate. The photographer elicits smiles, if not at the start, then in time, once the lenses improve, once the apparatus becomes more familiar. The apparatus, or the photographer, requested at least the outward sign of a particular emotion, and often got it. Now the devices capture the emotion, interpreted out of a database of emotions that have been experienced somewhere, sometime, and they work with it. Video cameras that capture facial expressions and modes of attention migrate from the workplace to zones of leisure to the shopping centre to the school or other institutions. In June 2018, reports circulated of a 'smart classroom behaviour management system', used in a school to assess degrees of attention and mind wandering during classes through computerised facial analysis.[10] The company Amazon is a leader in deploying these measures of emotional and affective response in the workplace and in the arena of consumption. In September 2018, there were reports that Amazon had applied for a patent for self-opening smart parcels that can video the recipient's 'excitement' as they open the package'.[11] Emotional reactions

10. Kristin Houser, 'Not Paying Attention in Class? China's "Smart Eye" Will Snitch on You', *Future Society* (May, 2018) available, www.futurism.com/smart-eye-china-facial-recognition/

11. Marc Blunden, 'Smile for Amazon: Your Next Parcel Could Film Your Reaction as you Open the Box' (September, 2018) available, www.standard.co.uk/tech/amazon-parcels-film-reaction-a3941036.html#comments

can be logged as data useful to future sales or sold back to the buyer as part of the service.

There is plenty of emotional work to do. Through the device, this emotional work can produce value inside and outside of what is obviously a workplace. Ours are emoji times, in which we are constantly required – or invited – to indicate our emotional state. Our personal atmosphere is logged. Familiar faces invite us to press them after passing through security at an airport, in shopping malls, cafés or banks. The company Happy or Not, who manufactures push button technology and the analytic software to process it, has the strapline 'Creating happiness in every business, worldwide'. It provides Smiley Face feedback technologies for employees too. Consumers click 'like' buttons, or more likely a thumbs up, a heart, or a sad face. In 2016, Facebook rolled out a palette of 'Reactions' to click on in response to posts – thereby producing quantifiable data. Alongside 'Like' there were 'Love' 'Haha', 'Wow' 'Sad' and 'Angry'. Social media – those formats that have insinuated themselves into our waking lives at all points and are entwined with advertising – collate emotions; results of pressing icons of love, sadness and surprise in reaction to so many tiny events, all day, into the night. Emotions take on a thing or image form. They become emblematic, like the original device, but not as a mark of a particular belonging, more a generic one. They adopt an alienated and standardised existence. There may be a bias towards the positive, as in Facebook. If the posts are to be resources for advertisers, then they must maximise their circulation. Negative emotions, some argue, are less likely to be 'shared', and so all this positivity keeps the consumers online, on board and on message[12], while it feeds

12. Kevan Lee, 'Buffer Social Blog' (October, 2015) available, www.blog.bufferapp.com/positivity-social-media

into the algorithmic organisation of 'stories' and targeted advertising, and as our private inner feelings are broadcast publicly and to entities way beyond our ken and for ends we can barely fathom. Perhaps there are historical shifts in this emotional landscape. Social media is the dominant channel of everyday life and thus registers so much everyday injustice. More recently, in these fraught times of social division and discord, it has been asserted that: 'Negative emotions like outrage and contempt and anxiety tend to drive significantly more engagement than positive ones'.[13]

SELF-RECKONING

Emotions in the digital age are tracked, monitored, packaged, analysed, and sometimes sold off elsewhere as data. Emotions are a part of a human package including what has come to be called 'the quantified self', a self intertwined with – subject to, but also compliant with – tracking and archiving. This quantified self is a natural inhabitant of the 'Quantified Workplace' and was first engendered in relation to medical and fitness technologies, such as Fitbit devices or other fitness trackers. It was propelled into wider visibility through events in Silicon Valley, organised by Kevin Kelly of *Wired* and the journalist Gary Wolf, who were promoting what has now come to be a worldwide movement with digitally and physically organised groups who explore 'self knowledge through numbers'.[14] What begins as a curiosity

13. Mark O'Connell, 'The Deliberate Awfulness of Social Media', *The New Yorker*, (September, 2018) available, www.newyorker.com/books/ under-review/the-deliberate-awfulness-of-social-media

14. Deborah Lupton, *The Quantified Self: A Sociology of Self-tracking* (Cambridge: Polity Press, 2016) and Phoebe V. Moore, *The Quantified Self in Precarity? Work, Technology and What Counts* (London: Routledge, 2017).

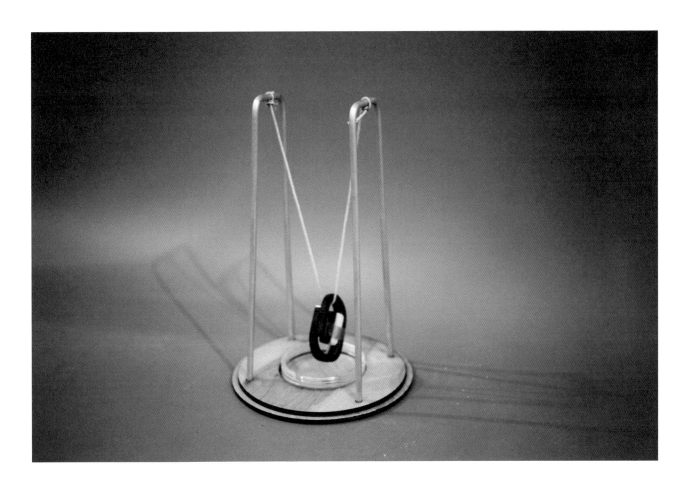

Tega Brain and Surya Mattu, *Unfit Bits*, 2015

Tega Brain and Surya Mattu, *Unfit Bits*, 2015

about oneself in terms of fitness, well-being, sleep quality, bodily capacities, becomes a gamified and ideologised quest for self-care, self-management and self-optimisation, which is seen to make especial sense in a climate or atmosphere in which there exists competition for work and, once employed, the injunction to beat targets, while the wider world promises only exposure to eroded medical care, dismantled welfare states and the widespread nature of anxiety.[15] Personal wellness is the responsibility of each and must be attended to through tracking and logging – well-being is not to be conceived of as the result of structural deficiencies in the workplace or the social realm. Self-knowledge, in the face of the dysfunctional state and irresponsible workplace, exists alongside the simultaneous production of knowledge for others, in the form of big data, which our devices give up continually.

There is now the widespread adoption of GPS and bio-tracking devices. Employees freely grasp to the integration of the device into the body or self, making their data voluntarily available as involuntary capacity. At Three Square Market, a self-service vending machine manufacturer, 50 employees voluntarily accepted RFID microchips to be inserted into their bodies in 2017.[16] Its initial uses were for banal activities such as unlocking doors, logging in to computers, using printers, buying snacks, and storing photos, bitcoins, living wills and the like. The company is working on adding GPS functionality and gaining body

15. WHO (World Health Organization) 'Investing in Treatment for Depression and Anxiety Leads to Fourfold Return', (April, 2016) available, www.who.int/en/news-room/detail/13-04-2016-investing-in-treatment-for-depression-and-anxiety-leads-to-fourfold-return
16. Rachel Metz, 'MIT Technology Review' (August, 2018) www.technologyreview.com/s/611884/this-company-embeds-microchips-in-its-employees-and-they-love-it/

data for medical and health purposes, data that might be of interest to HR as well as companies, governments and others. The chip's capacities will extend in the future. In November 2018, reports circulated in the UK press of the widening presence of microchips in workers and the Trades Union Congress and the Confederation of British Industry voiced concerns about control and micromanagement.[17] The self is screened. The self is a screen. The workers become their own devices. They become devices of a highly communicative capitalism.

This text is based in part on 'This Other Atmosphere: Against Human Resources, Emoji, and Devices', *Journal of Visual Culture*, Vol.18, No.1 (April, 2019).

Esther Leslie is Co-director of the Birkbeck Institute for the Humanities. Her recent books include *Derelicts: Thought Worms from the Wreckage* (Unkant, 2014), *Liquid Crystals: The Science and Art of a Fluid Form* (Reaktion, 2016) and, with Melanie Jackson, *Deeper in the Pyramid* (Banner Repeater, 2018).

17. Bjorn Larsson Rosvall, 'Microchip Implants Are Threatening Workers' Rights', *The Conversation* (November, 2018) available, theconversation.com/microchip-implants-are-threatening-workers-rights-107221

Kelly Richardson, *Glow*, 1998
HD video, seamless loop; Installation view: Albright-Knox Art Gallery

Sam Meech, *Punchcard Economy*, 2013
Knitted cotton, 5m × 3m (and detail)

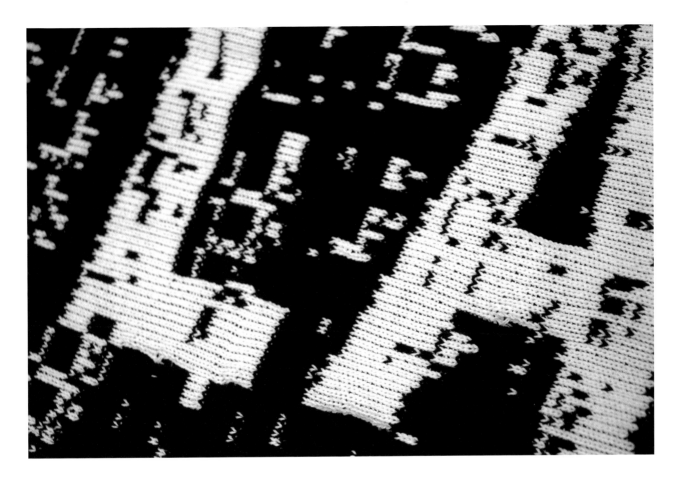

The text within the collage reads:

OP I found you
it's just... to
Stop asking
Peel off the judging
It worries me OLOT
productive w

Erica Scourti, *Difficult to Find the Lost Things* (detail), 2019

SEEKING EFFORTLESS ATTENTION

Malcolm McCullough

To go out for a walk should be enough of a start. Being present in public space remains the most basic civic act. If something is discouraging this, then the arts must resist it. An arts venue might ask you to sit and stay, and to watch or listen, but first off it asks you to be there. For if there is not even time for public space, much less for reading texts about them, then how is one to feel like a citizen? An occasional happening may help, and recent mobilisations make viral news, but indeed a better city life is always being collectively enacted. All this is obvious enough, especially in London, where of all places, notions of walks, publics and commons remain points of pride. Yet this timeless reality seems newly relevant to anyone seeking sense amid the pressures of 24/7 connectivity. To recall it might even justify a few moments of your time here.

Let this reading be something about settings. But this is not about paying attention to your surroundings. You probably have little more attention to pay. Instead, if this essay can remind you to use the word 'attention' without always preceding it with the word 'pay', then the moments of your time will have been worthwhile.

What does it take to find a more effortless attention for one another in a public space, such as Somerset House? After all, the places which afford such awareness have always been the heart of the good city life. Cities provide (and must also somehow regulate) places that reward but do not demand attention. If those places are now full of people being led about by their smartphones, this obviously takes some shift in sensibilities. This too seems obvious enough. Yet among the millions of citizens pondering this shift, and even here among dozens of select artists provoking such rethinking, too few ask what makes attention effortless, and not always something to *pay*. Fewer still ask where.

For an example of fluent but undemanding practice, note how city dwellers (and again, Londoners especially) tend to be masters of 'civil inattention'[1]: the art of noticing and accommodating one another without ever appearing to do so. To this sensibility, eye contact would be a clumsy gaffe. Otherwise unnoticed itself, this practice deserves note, since some great cultural category error seems to have occurred. Not appearing to notice one another is not the same as losing awareness of the very existence of one another!

In accompaniment to a superb set of art works about always-on city life, in that most public and historic of art spaces, Somerset House, this essay invites a few moments of reflection on civil inattention in shared surroundings.

1. Erving Goffman, *Relations in Public: Microstudies of the Public Order* (Harmondsworth: Penguin, 1972).

If 24/7 has disrupted *when* (attention is payed, demanded, with civility or not?), you might ask something different about *where*.

Distraction engineering surely has become the baseline condition. Yet almost nobody attests how much better life was before that horrid Google. Almost nobody wants to be tethered to a landline, stuck in an office, on somebody else's schedule. Instead, since work has left the office and gone 24/7, attention management has become an ever more vital existential challenge. In this, it is worth reciting two familiar analogies: cars and food. Back in the mid-20th century, people tried doing pretty much everything in cars (imagine a drive-in funeral home for instance). Cities remade (and soon enough damaged) themselves to keep the cars moving. But then the infatuations and advantages wore off. By now people know some things are better done without cars, and more walkable neighbourhoods are in higher demand. By contrast, the food analogy is more long-term. For thousands of years, salt, fat and sugar were almost always scarce, and hence the instinct is to almost always take them on. Except now they are not scarce. So too for bright colours, clever iconography, and incoming messages. Always scarce until lately, they lead into overconsumption. That then spirals into decreasing satisfaction with ever emptier calories. You know that, of course, but may still reach for the digital sweets and savouries.

A disclaimer seems necessary. Information overload has always existed too. If, per the cognitive truism, you can keep seven things in mind at once, then there has been overload ever since there were eight. Yet something quite important has changed. Never has so much of the sensory environment has been placed to appeal. Never before has

ARTIST INTERVIEW

Alexandra Daisy Ginsberg

Artist exploring science, technology, nature, and the design of living matter.

What is your relationship to 24/7 culture (as evidenced by the ceaselessness of contemporary capitalism)?

Probably like everyone, I'm overwhelmed by the intense and mounting pressure of contributing 24/7; clocking in and clocking up emails, likes, check-ins. How do we manage expectations as we allow more to come at us, ever faster? I want to think beyond the unending demand and give attention to other organisms that are affected by our choice to submit to 24/7 capitalism.

How do you work/sleep/play (keeping in the mind the old adage of '8 hours of work, 8 hours of rest, 8 hours of what we will')?

With intense desire to escape the treadmill, but with uncertainty at what lies at its edges, as we are told to never look down.

What does art have to do with this (or, what do you want your artistic practice to communicate about life/technology/time today and in the future)?

I try to bring things into focus that we might not otherwise notice. I'm using a technology that is helping drive this acceleration to reconstruct something that we are in danger of losing, but are barely aware of. Birds are affected by our increasing noise and light pollution. Using machine learning to reconstruct a synthetic dawn chorus – replacing the chorus to bring attention to its loss – may be perverse, but perhaps that dark humour might make us pause, and reflect on our actions.

SEEKING EFFORTLESS ATTENTION

even half so much of the cultural experience been reverse engineered for cognition. While not the moment to moralise on overconsumption, do let us at least acknowledge it. This is how it is now.

Today's prevailing cultural rants seldom separate these individual tendencies from the powers that induce and monetise them. For context, note a few prevalent memes. At the moment the favoured epithet is 'surveillance capitalism'.[2] Where the subjects seem willing, these corporate practices also overlap with what is often called the 'quantified self'.[3] With so much happening right this moment, or fed from moments ago, or offering instant gratification, anything *not* immediate falls from consideration; the 24/7 condition has also been called 'present shock'.[4] Wherever that gets monetised, look for the 'attention merchants'.[5] For one of the better works on how this demands metaphysical choice, admit the 'distraction addiction'.[6]

All those phenomena worsen without grounding in context. Anyone who lacks worthwhile surroundings, even just a window to gaze from, but preferably a place to walk among fellow citizens, is all the more vulnerable to overconsuming feeds from afar. Tuning out the chaos and din of the

2. Shoshana Zuboff, *The Age of Surveillance Capitalism: The Fight for a Human Future at the New Frontier of Power* (New York: PublicAffairs, 2019).
3. Gary Wolf and Kevin Kelly, 'Know Thyself: Tracking Every Facet of Life, from Sleep to Mood to Pain, 24/7/365', (June, 2009) www.wired.com/2009/06/lbnp-knowthyself/
4. Douglas Rushkoff, *Present Shock: When Everything Happens Now* (New York: Penguin, 2013).
5. Tim Wu, *The Attention Merchants: The Epic Scramble to Get Inside Our Heads* (New York: Knopf, 2016).
6. Alex Soojung-Kin Pang, *The Distraction Addiction* (Boston: Little, Brown, 2013).

metropolis remains necessary, but so does tuning in to at least some surroundings, and not only to avoid being hit when you step into the road. The art of leaving space and dignity for one another is a deliberate cultural habit much more subtle than outright ignoring one another. Civil inattention cannot morph into narcissistic oblivion.

The reset isn't overnight. Something different might trigger it for each of us. You cannot be *against* technology, but you must not be *led about* by technology.

○　　　○　　　○

Someday may there be a better name, but for now let's admit the *'post-digital' condition*. This popular expression does not mean life after server stacks and smartphones. But it does bring a different awareness of them. Then while the usage nevertheless continues, the medium is no longer noteworthy in itself. Instead, the 'post-digital' condition reflects a desire for greater agency. Per the Dutch media critic Florian Cramer's oft-cited explanation, in this regard, 'postdigital is a bit like [...] postcolonial.'[7] Thus to a great many artists today, urban subjectivity moves beyond infatuation with the platforms and instead toward revealing their assumed workings. This may involve a conscious readmission, although not Luddite retreat into, preexisting media and practices too. But mainly it cultivates a new fondness for the revelatory glitches, intermittencies, and appropriations, of the purportedly anywhere/always enticements. At least that's what many more observers besides artists are saying.

7. Florian Cramer, 'What is Postdigital?' in David Berry and Michael Dieter, eds., *Postdigital Aesthetics: Art, Computation, Design* (London: Palgrave McMillan, 2014).

Under these conditions, let's reconsider the value of *effortless attention* to surroundings.[8] That is what this essay is saying. This argument has three basic steps. First, attention need not be something you *pay*. (That seems a fitting claim here for *24/7*, given Jonathan Crary's work has also examined the notion of paid attention in the early origins of mass media.)[9] In counterpoint to the captive audience, today's usual emphasis is on participatory flow. As in art, sport, or good city life, attention can arise from habits, practices, and sensibilities, in a manner where more engagement is not more demanding, and fascination with this flow can reduce the impulse towards entertainment – or towards compulsive work-related communications. Second, not all that informs has been *sent*. The intrinsic structure, texture, and scale of surroundings informs as well. Third, to the extent that any such set of informative contexts of fascinating practices can be understood as a constituting a commons, it is mainly through *habits*. Let's consider these in turn.

Attention is the coin of the realm. As per the obligatory aphorism of cybernetic pioneer Herb Simon, attention is what becomes scarce when information becomes plentiful. Attention is not just a state, but a set of practices, and so just what to cultivate against informational overconsumption. As in many better practices, the goal is to get into the flow. Situated actions amid nameless affordances cultivate a quiet fascination. That is far more rewarding than furnished

8. Brian Bruya, *Effortless Attention: A New Perspective in the Cognitive Science of Attention and Action* (Cambridge MA: MIT Press, 2010).
9. Jonathan Crary, *Suspensions of Perception: Attention, Spectacle, and Modern Culture* (Cambridge, Mass.: MIT Press, 2001).

Catherine Richards, *Shroud / Chrysalis I*, 2000

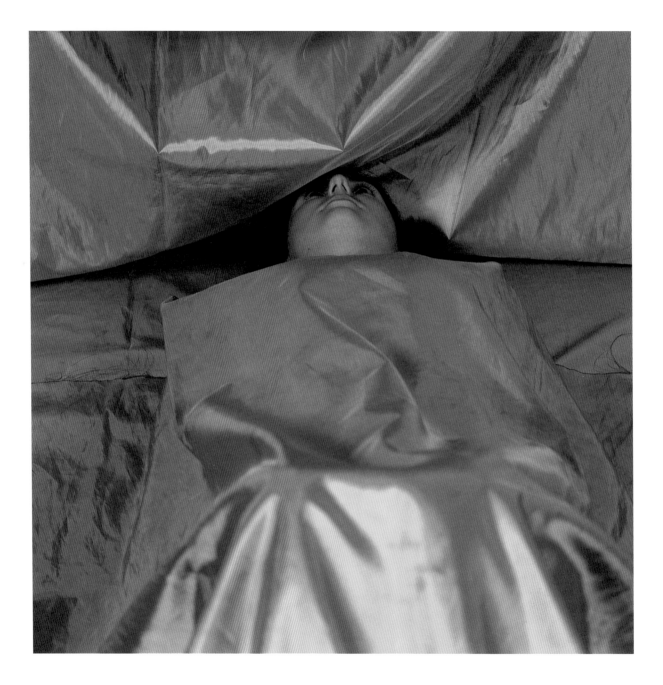

Catherine Richards, *Shroud / Chrysalis I*, 2000

entertainments or perpetual messaging. Ideally it becomes a reward in itself, and one more difficult for others to monetise.

Not all that informs has been sent. Like footprints in the snow, or the imprint of a head left on a pillow, traces of use inform without being intended as messages.

Conversely, even for transmitted messages, physical context disambiguates the interpretation. Without that, not all data transmissions inform. Context can shape which messages are noticed and welcome. A city in which you can act, speak, dress, or walk the same way anywhere and everywhere is not a very interesting one. Better that different sites would enact different practices and presences.

Physical scale has great strength in this role. The same event would feel very different indeed in a space half or twice as large. The scale of physical surroundings shapes the scale of interpersonal distances too. The perception of crowding depends very much on what people are doing, and who, and how often. Scale of course also communicates something about organisations and their aspirations. Scale needs dynamic range. A building in which all the ceilings were the same height would not be a very interesting one. This might all seem obvious, and yet on some strange new level of cultural category error, it is not. The relation between the handheld personal device and the vast distant cloud has become so powerful that the existence, much less the informative roles, of intermediate scales of physical space seem sometimes forgotten.

Third, habits shape such informative contextual sensibilities. Again, attention is a practice, or more specifically a set of practices. That is true for organisations, even communities, as well as individuals. For instance a city that addresses light pollution gets into the habit of noticing it.

There exist not only habits of information ethics, but also etiquettes, policies, even laws. A neighbourhood that restricts electronic billboards somehow values shared surroundings. It has many small habits and transactions of keeping watch. It recognises the costs of intrusions that do not share local priorities. While a business has a right to advertise itself, it might not have the right to do so on the doorways to city hall, nor with loudspeakers in the night. While a tourist has a right to take a picture, there might be practical limits to how many tourists may do so simultaneously. While the police have a right to keep watch on a street, there would be something odd about them reading every person's devices passively, as if everywhere is a checkpoint. And while the ironically blasé urban subject has the need and desire to tune something out and something else in, a city where everyone only heard their own playlists, and gazed only at their own curated handheld feeds, could become quite dull, or worse. The individual habit of assuming that the world around you is not very interesting could become culturally self-fulfilling at urban scale. It might also lead to an imbalance of entertainment and fascination, and hence to a crime wave of corporate attention theft. So it is an important habit to be here now.

Suffice it to say that one word often found in such situations is *commons*. What do you call a context in which enough participants tune in and not out? What kinds of places depend on many small but collective actions? Where does that occur without branded identity, subscribing members, or ticketed program? This is obviously an important and difficult question. You might as well ask what makes citizens identify with favourite places in the city, and again, how different that is from having the identity declared and sold to them. How do practices arise outside the mechanisms of

Liam Young, *Renderlands*, 2017
(Film stills of digital utopia constructed from scavenged 3D models, Los Angeles)

Liam Young, *Renderlands*, 2017
(Film stills of an outsourced animation studio, Bangalore, India)

a market or the programmes of a state? Why are ad-hoc and hyperlocal organisations so important to urban resource networks? Where does a set of collective agreements about activity at street level constitute some kind of temporary commons? These are questions for political economists, information ethicists, and environmental educators alike, as well as artists.

A commons is probably not what you think it is. To speak of it won't get you dismissed as a romantic. When is a commons not tragic? How is it not a preindustrial meadow, nor a branding misnomer (as in so many real estate names), nor a naive socialist aspiration? For here the most usual misconception is that any commons, whatever it is, will suffer free-riding and 'drawdown'. That is the usual meaning of the tragedy of the commons (which alas is all that many business strategists feel they need to recite, dismissively, on the matter) – that each inside participant takes too much and inadvertently depletes it. Or worse, that outside forces will privatise the good parts and pollute the rest. Yet it need not always be so.

As the political economy of sufficiency can explain, (see Lewis Hyde's *Common as Air,* for one)[10], a pooled but unmanaged resource with insufficient communications among participants really isn't a commons at all. A true commons has enough practices of making rounds, using only intermittently, and recognising overconsumption, so that it can maintain itself against drawdown. While the economists' usual examples may be in, say, fisheries or watersheds, examples exist in informational practice too. While more usual notions of informational commons tend to be online and often about cornucopias (with Wikipedia the

10. Lewis Hyde, *Common As Air: Revolution, Art, and Ownership* (London: Union Books, 2012).

immediate example), other kinds of informational commons can exist in urban space too. And indeed they must: surely some information ethics must exist at street level, and some habits of maintaining something shared needs enactment.

For instance, practices in managing outdoor screens, abating noise pollution, or designating areas for tobacco do exist and do provide cultural, even economic benefits. From a political perspective, and with interesting implications for other information media at street level, signage law seems the most interesting of these, for it is no mere censorship. To treat data streams as pollution quickly gets complicated. After all, one person's signal is another person's noise. What was noise to you a minute ago might become signal after some shift of intent. Yet these are often matters of degree. For example signage law distinguishes items that refer elsewhere versus items that describe the site on which they appear. Such by-laws are interested in scale, and also in spatial frequency. They enact some larger truth about being allowed to say your bit, but not to drown the others out. They understand civil inattention.

All told, out in the spaces of an increasingly information-rich city, some new spectrum of attitudes must arise. The informative role of physical context itself must be recognised and upheld. Part individual sensibility, part media etiquette, part collective awareness, sometimes on-site policy, and sometimes local law, this consensual new attitude helps reset conditions away from the early infatuations with perpetual connectivity. Individually, it arises in willing presence; collectively, it shows up in agreed patterns of actions. *How* it does, will require the best of philosophers, social critics, and artists to guide. Whether or not it implies or enacts a commons, it certainly upholds inhabitable scale. As the infatuation wears off from the present shock of devices and clouds, these notions of grounding in place may yet help, and their slippages and glitches invite new forms of art. The point is to rediscover habits of attention to other people in fascinating places, and to enjoy them as an ultimately effortless practice, not as one more demand of the kinds of attention one is too often asked to pay. Such habits do seem to need a reset, amid conditions of perpetual messaging, non-stop entertainment, and 24/7 predations of work. Since there is never time, this reset can begin anytime. Just step out the door...

August 2019, Ann Arbor Michigan, USA

Malcolm McCullough is Professor of Architecture at Taubman College of Architecture and Urban Planning at the University of Michigan, where he teaches architecture and media arts. McCullough is the author of *Downtime on the Microgrid* (forthcoming 2020); *Ambient Commons* (2013); *Digital Ground* (2004); and *Abstracting Craft* (1996).

Susan Hiller, *Dream Mapping*, 1974
Composite Dream Map

Susan Hiller, *Dream Mapping*, 1974
Participants sleeping in a field at Purdies Farm, Hampshire

Tyler Coburn, *Professional Nonproducer*, 2011
Interior house paint, 10 × 15 cm

AFTERWORD

Jonathan Crary

In the half decade since *24/7* was published, the crisis it outlined has clearly worsened. The looming likelihood of climate catastrophe has heightened a general awareness of the contradiction the book articulated: the fundamental and corrosive incompatibility between human life and the systemic imperatives of 21st century capitalism. We live amidst the non-stop hyperactivity of production, consumption, extraction, transport and circulation, occurring on a global scale, all fuelled by processes of accumulation, of possessiveness, by artificially contrived appetites that are intrinsically unappeasable. The speed and ubiquity of digital networks amplifies, for billions of people, the incontestable priority of getting, having, owning, coveting, envying, all of which inflames the restlessness of the world, operating without pause, without the possibility of rest or recovery, a world choking on its heat and waste. Regrettably, most of the many projects and industries of renewable energy are undertaken for perpetuating business as usual, with all

its devastating patterns of growth and development.
Any schemes for emission reduction are futile unless the
senseless acquisitiveness, the compulsive expenditure,
the global industries of resource appropriation and
military domination incited by neoliberal capitalism can be
switched off. As some critics have remarked, whether we
get enough sleep now is the least of our worries.

I would contend, however, that the issue of sleep is as
important as ever, if it can be understood as a figure for
the rhythms and cycles, for the interludes of stillness and
regeneration that are essential for our collective survival
and for all living systems. The human need for alternations
of waking and sleeping, of work and recuperation is
mirrored in current environmental unravelings produced
by 24/7 exploitation and exhaustion. One of the features
of a free market economy is the irrelevance of any notion
of preservation or conservation. Take the example of the
long undeveloped Yasuni rain forest in Ecuador, home for
thousands of years to an indigenous population but also
rich in crude oil under the ground. When the government
of Rafael Correa proposed in 2007 that no drilling would
take place if a global fund of a mere 3.6 billion dollars
could be raised to compensate the nation for the sacrifice
of oil revenues, the wealthiest institutions on earth, over
five years, could barely come up with a pledges totalling
a few million dollars. Now drilling, road building and
deforestation is ongoing there around the clock. The
lesson: if there are monetisable resources of any kind to
be extracted anywhere, they will be. All over the planet
now there is a frenzied spree of plundering, whether as
fracking, coal mining, offshore drilling, industrial farming,
toxic mineral refining, and the polluting of oceans and
rivers. This massive looting and devastation proceeds
without pause and without limits, destroying the life cycles
and biodiversity of complex environments. All our new

digital technologies, robotics, electric vehicles, quantum computing, head mounted displays and so on depend on the capture of raw materials from the global south but also on the political forms of control and military terror, including the creation of failed states, that are necessary to accomplish this.

In retrospect, part of my book's subtitle (*the Ends of Sleep*) was susceptible to misunderstanding. Instead of suggesting the idea of an 'end' as purpose, goal, aim, to some it seemed as if I was gloomily announcing the advent of a sleepless world. Rather, I was proposing that a primary end or purpose of sleep is rest, withdrawal, quiescence, all of which oppose the demands of 24/7 capitalism. So for me it is source of optimism that there are aspects of human and social life that are effectively unconquerable by the forces of financialisation and commodification. Capitalism can damage and despoil our interludes of sleep and repose, but in fact there are unsurpassable limits that resist its seemingly inexorable tendencies and dismantle the absurd predictions that we are evolving into bio-mechanical hybrids.

While the intensification of global warming and its outcomes now seem the most disastrous consequence of 24/7 temporalities, these are equally injurious to the fabric of social life and civil society. 24/7 poses the delusion of a time without waiting, of an on-demand instantaneity, of getting and having, while insulated from the physical presence of others and any sense of mutual responsibility that might be entailed. 24/7 also undermines the individual patience and deference that are crucial to all forms of direct democracy – the patience to listen to others and to wait one's turn to speak. 24/7 is the relentless conversion of every possible interval of time or every form of social interaction into the values of the marketplace. It is a condition of permanent exposure and illumination in which nothing can remain hidden or private. The precariousness and uprootedness of current conditions of labour and the disintegration of long standing forms of social solidarity are inseparable from the epidemics of depression, addiction, suicide and mass murder.

Realistic strategies of resistance require the invention of new ways of living. There has to be a radical rethinking of what our needs are, of rediscovering our own desires beyond the flood of destructive and shallow cravings that are promoted unremittingly. Not only must we stop buying what we are told we need, we must disavow the role of consumer altogether. There must be a refusal of the deathliness of billionaire culture, and all the debilitating images of ownership and material affluence with which we're surrounded. For those with children, it means abandoning the many desperate expectations they now carry to compete for individual success, and instead providing them with anticipations of a livable future shared in common. But these changes would be just the beginning, preliminary to the larger and more difficult challenges ahead.

These are tasks that cannot be imposed from above by existing institutions or programmed by 'experts'. As this exhibition strongly suggests, artists will be at the forefront of crafting pathways that lead us out of the deteriorating political circumstances of the present. Many current art practices point toward a hybrid material culture based on both old and new improvised techniques of living and subsisting cooperatively. The visionary and pragmatic capabilities of artists will be crucial for the reorganisation of cities, for the reclaiming of derelict spaces and broken ecosystems, for fashioning new uses for existing tools and materials, for reconceiving the bonds between humans and animals, and for the amelioration of psychic and social fragmentation.

September 2019, New York

Jonathan Crary is an art critic and essayist, and is Meyer Schapiro Professor of Modern Art and Theory at Columbia University in New York.

Nastja Säde Rönkkö, *6 Months Without*, 2018–2019

BIBLIOGRAPHY

EXHIBITION OBJECT LIST

Armitage, John, *Paul Virilio: From Modernism to Hypermodernism and Beyond* (London: Sage, 2000).

Armitage, John, and Roberts, Joanne, *Living with Cyberspace: Technology and Society in the 21st Century* (New York: Continuum, 2003).

Bauman, Zygmunt, *Globalization: The Human Consequences* (New York: Columbia University Press, 1998).

Bauman, Zygmunt, *Liquid Modernity* (London: Blackwell, 2000).

Benjamin, Walter, 'The Work of Art in the Age of its Technological Reproducibility' (2nd version), in *The Work of Art in the Age of Its Technological Reproducibility and Other Writings on Media*, eds. Michael W. Jennings, Bridget Doherty and Thomas Levin, trans. Michael W. Jennings (Harvard University Press, Cambridge, MA, 2008).

All works as of 1 September 2019.

WRECKAGE OF THE DAY

NONE Collective
J3RR1. A Planned Torture, 2017 (p.36)
Lighting equipment composed of electronic and informatic technologies, aluminium foil, mirrors, filament lamps, 25 solenoids
© NONE Collective
Courtesy of the artist

Roman Signer
BETT, 5. Dezember 1996, 1996 (p.64–65)
Single channel video projection
4:15 mins
Pilot: Armin Caspari
Video: Aleksandra Signer
Courtesy of Roman Signer and Hauser & Wirth

Joseph Wright of Derby (1734–1797)
Arkwright's Cotton Mills by Night, ca.1790s (p.11)
Oil on canvas
Private Collection, UK

UBERMORGEN
Chinese Coin (Red Blood), 2015 (p.43)
Mixed-media installation, full HD video
Courtesy of the artist
Originally commissioned by NEoN Digital Arts

EXHIBITION OBJECT LIST

Étienne Jules Marey
Chronophotograph of 'Chat chute' or cat falling,
1890–1894
Modern print from original celluloid negative film
Courtesy of Science Museum Group

Rut Blees Luxemburg
A Modern Project (Highrise), 1995 (p.12)
C-type on Aluminium
Courtesy of the artist

Rut Blees Luxemburg
Narrow Stage, 1998 (p.66)
C-type on Aluminium
Courtesy of the artist

Julia Varela
X/5.000, 2017 (p.44)
Series of folded TV plasma screens
Courtesy of the artist

Marcus Coates
Self Portrait as Time, 2016 (p.6)
Digital video, continual duration (12 hour loop)
Courtesy of the artist, Kate MacGarry and
Workplace Gallery

Unknown Maker (France)
Empire Type World Clock (for indicating time
around the globe), 1909 (p.77)
Patentee: Etienne de Gounevitch and Armand
Gustave Couaillett
Brass, metal, paper
Courtesy of Science Museum Group

Kimchi & Chips
Bucheon Incinerator (Now B39), Part of *Lunar
Surface,* 2014
KR Digital photo print
In collaboration with photographer
Eunyoung Kim
Courtesy of the artist

Benjamin Grosser
ORDER OF MAGNITUDE, 2019
HD video with stereo audio
47:15 mins
Courtesy of the artist

BIBLIOGRAPHY

Beloff, Zoe, *Emotions Go To Work* (Colchester: Minor Compositions, 2018).

Benjamin, Marina, *Insomnia* (Waterville, Maine: Thorndike Press, 2019).

Blunden, Marc, 'Smile for Amazon: Your Next Parcel Could Film Your Reaction as you Open the Box' (September, 2018) available, www.standard.co.uk/tech/amazon-parcels-film-reaction-a3941036.html#comments

Boden, Margaret, ed., *The Philosophy of Artificial Intelligence* (Oxford: Oxford University Press, 1990).

Bridle, James, *New Dark Age: Technology and the End of the Future* (London & New York: Verso, 2019).

Brown, Wendy, 'Neoliberalized Knowledge', *History of the Present*, Vol.1, No.1 (Summer, 2011) p.113–129.

Bruya, Brian, *Effortless Attention: A New Perspective in the Cognitive Science of Attention and Action* (Cambridge MA: MIT Press, 2010).

Brynjolfsson, Erik, *The Second Machine Age: Work, Progress, and Prosperity in a Time of Brilliant Technologies,* ed. Andrew McAfee (Vancouver, B.C: Langara College, 2018).

Carey, James W., *Communication as Culture: Essays on Media and Society* (New York: Routledge, 1989).

Cramer, Florian, 'What is Postdigital?' in David Berry and Michael Dieter, eds., *Postdigital Aesthetics: Art, Computation, Design* (London: Palgrave McMillan, 2014).

BIBLIOGRAPHY

Crary, Jonathan, *Suspensions of Perception: Attention, Spectacle, and Modern Culture* (Cambridge, Mass.: MIT Press, 2001).

Crary, Jonathan, *24/7: Late Capitalism and the Ends of Sleep* (New York; London: Verso, 2014).

Duchenne de Boulogne, G.-B., *The Mechanism of Human Facial Expression* (Cambridge: Cambridge University Press, (1862) 2006).

Eden, Frederic Morton, *The State of the Poor: A History of the Labouring Classes in England, with Parochial Reports*, ed. A.G.L. Rogers (London: George Routledge & Sons, 1928).

Enthoven, Daniel, 'Quantified Self? How About A Quantified Workplace?' (2013) available, www.wired.com/insights/2013/05/quantified-self-how-about-a-quantified-workplace

Fuller, Matthew, *How to Sleep: The Art, Biology and Culture of Unconsciousness* (London & New York: Bloomsbury Academic, 2018).

Gabe, Jonathan, Williams, Simon J. and Coveney, Catherine M., 'Prescription Hypnotics in the News: A Study of UK Audiences', *Social Science & Medicine*, Vol.174 (1 February 2017) p.43–52.

Galison, Peter, *Einstein's Clocks, Poincare's Maps: Empires of Time* (New York: W. W. Norton and Company, 2003).

Glennie, Paul and Thrift, Nigel, *Shaping the Day: A History of Timekeeping in England and Wales, 1300–1800* (Oxford: Oxford University Press, 2009).

Ted Hunt
Sense of Time, 2018
Wear OS App installed on smart watch
Courtesy of the artist
A collaboration with King's College London's
Department of Philosophy, supported by the
Cultural Institute at King's in partnership with
Somerset House Studios
With support from the Adonyeva Foundation

SLEEP / ATTENTIVENESS

Kelly Richardson
Glow, 1998 (p.115)
HD video (remastered)
Courtesy of the artist

Tatsuo Miyajima
Life Palace (tea room), 2013 (p.15)
L.E.D., IC, microcomputer by Ikegami program,
wood, steel, passive sensor, electric wire, LED
type; Life G-BL 152 pieces ©Tatsuo Miyajima
Courtesy of Lisson Gallery

Iain Forsyth and Jane Pollard
Somnoproxy, 2019
Audio installation
13:00 mins
The Island courtesy of L'Acoustics
Story by Stuart Evers
Read by Enzo Cilenti and Kate Ashfield
Originally commissioned by Moog Sound Lab UK
With support from the Adonyeva Foundation

Alan Warburton
Sprites I-IV, 2019 (p.18–19)
Lenticular print
Courtesy of the artist
With support from the Adonyeva Foundation

Alice Vandeleur Boorer
Jet Slag: Around the World in 7 Sleeps, 2010 (p.60)
Documentary evidence of participation in
scientific 'Jet Lag' research
Courtesy of the artist

EXHIBITION OBJECT LIST

Ed Fornieles
Sleeping, 2015 (p.52)
HD Video, mp4
3:00 mins
Courtesy of the artist and Daata Editions

Adam Chodzko
Sleepers. Hole, 2012 (p.50–51)
Punctured found 35mm slides, C-type
Courtesy of the artist

Erica Scourti
Difficult to Find the Lost Things, 2019 (p.118)
Mixed media
Courtesy of the artist
Commissioned by Somerset House with support
from the Adonyeva Foundation

Esmeralda Kosmatopoulos
Fifteen Pairs of Mouths, 2016–19 (p.94–95)
Plaster, steel
Courtesy of the artist

Hasan Elahi
Scorpion W2, 2019 (p.78–79)
Translucent pigment prints on lightbox
Courtesy of the artist

Thomson & Craighead
Beacon, 2007
Modified railway flap sign, computer
Courtesy of the artists

Nastja Säde Rönkkö
6 Months Without, 2018–2019 (p.142)
Performance, HD-video, text, durational
intervention
Courtesy of the artist
Originally commissioned by Somerset House
Studios with support from the Adonyeva
Foundation, Wysing Arts Centre and
The Finnish Institute in London

BIBLIOGRAPHY

Goffman, Erving, *Relations in Public: Microstudies of the Public Order* (Harmondsworth: Penguin, 1972).

Griffiths, Jay, *A Sideways Look at Time* (New York: Putnam, 1999).

Haraway, Donna, *When Species Meet* (Minneapolis: University of Minnesota Press, 2008).

Hardt, Michael and Negri, Antonio, *Empire* (Cambridge, MA: Harvard University Press, 2000).

Hassan, Robert, *The Chronoscopic Society: Globalization, Time, and Knowledge in the Network Economy* (New York: Peter Lang, 2003).

Houser, Kristin, 'Not Paying Attention in Class? China's "Smart Eye" Will Snitch on You', *Future Society* (May, 2018) available, www.futurism.com/smart-eye-china-facial-recognition

Hyde, Lewis, *Common As Air: Revolution, Art, and Ownership* (London: Union Books, 2012).

Imai, Masaaki, *Gemba Kaizen: A Commonsense, Low-Cost Approach to Management* (New York: Mcgraw Hill, 1997).

Kern, Stephen, *The Culture of Time and Space 1880–1918* (Cambridge, MA: Harvard University Press, 1983).

Leader, Darian, 'Why the Sleep Industry is Keeping us Awake at Night', (March, 2019) www.theguardian.com/books/2019/mar/09/the-big-sleep-business-are-we-being-sold-an-impossible-dream

BIBLIOGRAPHY

Leibniz, Gottfried Wilhelm, 'Principles of Nature and Graces, based on Reason' (1714), in *Philosophical Texts*, trans. Richard Francks and R.S. Woolhouse (Oxford: Oxford University Press, 1998).

Lipovetsky, Giles, *Hypermodern Times*, trans. Andrew Brown (Malden, MA: Polity, 2005).

Marx, Karl, *Capital: A Critique of Political Economy, Vol.1,* trans. B. Fowkes and D. Fernbach (London: Penguin, (1867) 2002).

Marx, Karl, *Grundrisse*, trans. Martin Nicolaus (London: Penguin, 2012).

Mazzucato, Mariana, 'Takers and Makers: Who are the Real Value Creators? Where Value Meets Profit Meets Economic Rent', (June, 2019) www.evonomics.com/value-of-everything-mariana-mazzucato

McCullough, Malcolm, *Ambient Commons: Attention in the Age of Embodied Information* (Cambridge, Mass: MIT Press, 2015).

Odell, Jenny, 'Notes from How to Do Nothing', transcript of a talk given at EYEO 2017 in Minneapolis, available, medium.com/@the_jennitaur/how-to-do-nothing-57e100f59bbb

Odell, Jenny, *How to Do Nothing: Resisting the Attention Economy* (Brooklyn, NY: Melville House, 2019).

Parkins, Wendy and Craig, Geoffrey, *Slow Living* (Sydney: University of New South Wales University Press, 2006).

Pettman, Dominic, *Infinite Distraction* (Malden, MA: Polity, 2016).

○

ACCELERATION / SURVEILLANCE / CONTROL

Big Brother Diary Room Chair, Series 1, 2000
Courtesy of Alan Davies

Daniel Eatock
Big Brother Series 2 logo, 2001
Printed vinyl
Originally commissioned by Channel 4
Courtesy of the artist

Excerpts from *Big Brother*, Series 1, 2000
Courtesy of Courtesy of Endemol and Channel 4

Jeremy Bentham
A table of the springs of action: shewing the several species of pleasures and pains, of which man's nature is susceptible:... to which are added explanatory notes and observations, 1817 (p.4)
Bentham 2.T.4
Part of the Jeremy Bentham collection, UCL Special Collections
Courtesy of UCL Special Collections

Willey Reveley
Colour Drawing, After Bentham's Design, for the Panopticon, or Inspection House – a New Type of Prison, 1794 (p.12)
Drawing on paper with manuscript quotations
Bentham Papers 119 f.121
Courtesy of UCL Special Collections

Willey Reveley
Drawing, After Bentham's Design, for the Panopticon, or Inspection House – a New Type of Prison, 1791 (p.72)
Drawing, section and plan of the building
Bentham Papers 115 f.44
Courtesy of UCL Special Collections

Mark Thomas
Secure Beneath the Watchful Eyes, 2002
Poster
Courtesy of London Transport Museum

EXHIBITION OBJECT LIST

Pierre Huyghe
The Housing Projects, 2001 (p.71)
Video, projection, colour and sound (stereo)
7:51 mins
Tate: Presented by the Patrons of New Art
through the Tate Gallery Foundation 2003

Mat Collishaw
The Machine Zone 00:01, 2019
Animatronic sculpture, c-type prints
Courtesy of the artist

John Gerrard
Exercise (Dunhuang), 2014
Three custom made frameless brass screens,
computer, video
Courtesy of Borusan Contemporary, Istanbul

Biome Collective & Joseph DeLappe
Killbox, 2015–2016 (p.63)
Digital Interactive Installation
Courtesy of Biome Collective

Warwick Time Stamp Company
Time Recorder, ca.1890 (p.2)
Iron, brass, glass
Courtesy of Science Museum Group

Addie Wagenknecht
*Optimization of Parenthood, Part 2, Installation
Documentation*, 2012 (p.96)
Video (color, silent)
00:55 mins
Courtesy of the artist and bitforms gallery,
New York

Lawrence Lek
Play Station
Video
7:50 mins
Courtesy of the artist

BIBLIOGRAPHY

Pfaller, Robert, *Interpassivity: The Aesthetics of Delegated Enjoyment* (Edinburgh: Edinburgh University Press, 2017).

Postone, Moishe, *Time, Labor, and Social Domination: A Reinterpretation of Marx's Critical Theory* (New York: Cambridge University Press, 1993).

Rifkin, Jeremy, *Time Wars: The Primary Conflict in Human History* (New York: Simon and Schuster, 1987).

Rushkoff, Douglas, *Present Shock: When Everything Happens Now* (New York: Penguin, 2013).

Sandhu, Sukhdev, *Night Haunts: A Journey Through the London Night* (London: ArtAngel and Verso, 2007).

Sartre, Jean-Paul, *Nausea,* trans. Lloyd Alexander (New York: New Directions, 2013).

Scheuerman, William E., *Liberal Democracy and the Social Acceleration of Time* (Baltimore and London: Johns Hopkins University Press, 2004).

Schivelbusch, Wolfgang, *The Railway Journey: The Industrialization and Perception of Time and Space* (Berkeley: California University Press, 1987).

Sharma, Sarah, *In the Meantime: Temporality and Cultural Politics* (Durham, NC: Duke University Press, 2014).

Soojung-Kin Pang, Alex, *The Distraction Addiction* (Boston: Little, Brown, 2013).

Thompson, E.P., 'Time, Work, Discipline and Industrial Capitalism', *Past and Present,* Vol.38, (1967) p.56–97.

BIBLIOGRAPHY

Tomlinson, John, *The Culture of Speed: The Coming of Immediacy* (London: Sage, 2007).

Tronti, Mario, *Strategy of Refusal*, (1965), available, www.libcom.org/library/strategy-refusal-mario-tronti

Virilio, Paul, *Speed and Politics,* trans. Mark Polizzotti (New York: Semiotext(e), 1986).

Wajcman, Judy and Dodd, Nigel, eds., *The Sociology of Speed: Digital, Organizational, and Social Temporalities* (Oxford: Oxford Scholarship Online, 2016).

Wolf, Gary and Kelly, Kevin, 'Know Thyself: Tracking Every Facet of Life, from Sleep to Mood to Pain, 24/7/365', (June, 2009) www.wired.com/2009/06/lbnp-knowthyself/

Wu, Tim, *The Attention Merchants: The Epic Scramble to Get Inside Our Heads* (New York: Knopf, 2016).

Zuboff, Shoshana, *The Age of Surveillance Capitalism: The Fight for a Human Future at the New Frontier of Power* (New York: PublicAffairs, 2019).

○

WORK / THE COMMONS

John Butler
Xerox's Paradox, 2018 (p.85–86)
Digital prints
Courtesy of the artist
Originally commissioned by NEoN Digital Arts

Michel Mandiberg
Quantified Self Portrait (One Year Performance), 2016–17
3-channel HD video documenting a yearlong performance
Channels 1 and 2: 6:50 mins
Channel 3: 47:50 mins
Courtesy of the artist

Pilvi Takala
The Stroker, 2018 (p.101–102)
Two-channel video installation
14:26 mins
Courtesy of the artist

Harun Farocki (1944–2014)
Workers Leaving the Factory in 11 Decades, 2006
Video, 12 monitors, black and white and colour and sound (stereo)
42:26 mins
Tate: purchased using funds provided by the 2014 Outset / Frieze Art Fair Fund to benefit the Tate Collection 2015

British Time Recorder Company Limited
Time Recording Device used at the Central Telegraph Office, London, 1905 (p.105)
Cast iron, glass, paper, steel, wood
Courtesy of Science Museum Group

Alan Warburton
Dust Bunny, 2019
Dust collected from visual effects workstation computers
Courtesy of the artist
With support from the Adonyeva Foundation

Addie Wagenknecht
H4ckz for the beauty blogger in all of us,
2018–2019
YouTube Channel
Courtesy of the artist

Liam Young
Renderlands, 2017 (p.129–130)
Film of digital utopia constructed from
scavenged 3D models, 3D printed models
Courtesy of the artist

Tega Brain and Surya Mattu
Unfit Bits, 2015 (p.111–112)
Fit bit trackers, metronomes, Apple watch, bike
wheel, phone, phone swing, digital video
Courtesy of the artist

Kateřina Šedá
UNES-CO, 2018
Digital prints
Courtesy of the artist

Sam Meech
Punchcard Economy, 2013 (p.116–117)
Knitted cotton
Courtesy of the artist

RESET

Catherine Richards
Shroud / Chyrsalis I and II, 2000/2005
(p.125–126)
Glass table, copper taffeta/ metal, gels, paper
Shroud / Chyrsalis I courtesy of the Collection
of The Ottawa Art Gallery. Purchased with the
support of the Canada Council for the Arts
Acquisition Assistance program, Glen A. Bloom
and OAG's Acquisition Endowment Fund, 2004.
Shroud / Chyrsalis II courtesy of the artist

FURTHER READING

Bentham, Jeremy, *Deontology: Together with a Table of the Springs of Action; and the Article on Utilitarianism,* ed. Amnon Goldworth (Oxford; New York: Clarendon Press and Oxford University Press, 2002).

Bentham, Jeremy, *Panopticon: Or the Inspection House* (Whithorn: Anodos Books, (1791) 2017).

Bartlett, Jamie, *The People vs. Tech: How the Internet Is Killing Democracy (and How We Save It)* (New York: Dutton, 2018).

Berardi, Franco, *Breathing: Chaos and Poetry* (Los Angeles: Semiotext(e), 2019).

Biggs, Bryan, ed., *3am: Wonder, Paranoia and the Restless Night* (Liverpool: Liverpool University Press & The Bluecoat Gallery, 2013).

FURTHER READING

Blyth, Catherine, *On Time: Finding Your Pace in a World Addicted to Fast* (Glasgow: Harper Collins, 2017).

Bogdanov, Aleksandr, *Red Star: The First Bolshevik Utopia,* eds. Loren R Graham and Richard Stites, trans. Charles Rougle (Bloomington: Indiana Univ. Press, 2007).

Cohen, Kris, *Never Alone, Except for Now: Art, Networks, Populations* (Durham: Duke University Press, 2017).

Cohen, Josh, *Not Working: Why We Have to Stop* (London: Granta, 2018).

Colakides, Yiannis, Garrett, Marc and Gloerich, Inte, eds., *State Machines: Reflections and Actions at the Edge of Digital Citizenship, Finance, and Art* (Amsterdam: Institute of Network Cultures, 2019).

Cook, Sarah, *Information* (London; Cambridge, Massachusetts: Whitechapel Gallery, The MIT Press, 2016).

Cook, Sarah, ed., *Thomson & Craighead: Flat Earth* (Dundee and Memmingen: Dundee Contemporary Arts and MeWo Kunsthalle, 2013).

Cooper, Suzanne Fagence, *To See Clearly: Why Ruskin Matters* (London: Quercus, 2019).

Coupland, Douglas, *Microserfs* (Toronto: Harper Perennial, 2009).

Coupland, Douglas, *Player One: What Is to Become of Us* (London: William Heinemann, 2010).

Coupland, Douglas, *Machines Will Make Better Choices Than Humans* (Rotterdam: V2_, 2018).

Alexandra Daisy Ginsberg
Machine Auguries, 2019
Multi-channel sound installation
Machine Learning: Dr Przemek Witaszczyk (Faculty)
Sound design: Chris Timpson (Aurelia Soundworks)
Research/Design: Dr Alexandra Daisy Ginsberg, Johanna Just, Ness Lafoy, Ana Maria Nicolaescu
Lighting design: Lucy Carter
Associate to Lucy Carter: Sean Gleason
Production: Angharad Cooper
AV: KSO
With thanks to Chris Watson, Geoff Sample, The British Library, Sara Keen, Xeno-canto, Professor Ben Sheldon, Maria Diaz and Dr John Mansir of Faculty and Karishma Rafferty
Courtesy of the artist
Commissioned by Somerset House and A/D/O by MINI. With additional support from Faculty and the Adonyeva Foundation

Susan Hiller
Dream Mapping, 1974 (p.134–135)
Documentary reconstruction: facsimile dream maps and additional materials
© Estate of Susan Hiller
Courtesy of Lisson Gallery

Heath Bunting
Twin Charts, 2015–2017 (p.34–35)
Ink and pencil on paper
Courtesy of the artist

Tega Brain
An Orbit, 2016
Eccentric wireless router
Courtesy of the artist

Inés Cámara Leret
Photosphere, 2019
Synthesised light emitting silica combined with 291 grains of sand of diverse origins
Courtesy of the artist
Commissioned by Somerset House with support from the Adonyeva Foundation, IMDEA Materials Institute and Universidad La Rioja

EXHIBITION OBJECT LIST

Katie Paterson
As the World Turns, 2010
Adapted record player
Courtesy of the artist

Ted Hunt
Circa Solar, 2019
Wear OS App installed on smart watch
Courtesy of the artist
With support from the Adonyeva Foundation

Tyler Coburn
Professional Nonproducer, 2011 (p.136)
Farrow & Ball 'Blackened' and 'Hardwick White'
Reproduced by Rory Gallagher
Courtesy of the artist

Collection of Do Not Disturb Signs
Courtesy of Raoul Shah

Daily tous les jours
I Heard There Was a Secret Chord, 2017
Wood, metal, microphones, cables, computer,
software, speakers, frequencies
Original piece co-produced with the Musée d'Art
Contemporain de Montréal and the National
Film Board of Canada supported by the Canada
Council for the Arts' New Chapter program
Courtesy of the artists
With support from the Ministry of Culture in
Quebec

SITE WIDE / ONLINE / LIBRARY

Douglas Coupland
Slogans for the 21st Century, 2011–ongoing
(p.20, 27, 28, 32)
digital prints
Courtesy of the artist and Daniel Faria Gallery,
Toronto

Michel Mandiberg
Quantified Self Portrait (Rhythms), 2016–17
366-day audio file
Courtesy of the artist

FURTHER READING

Dick, Philip K., *Four Novels of the 1960s,* ed. Jonathan Lethem (New York: The Library of America, 2007).

Dick, Philip K., *Do Androids Dream of Electric Sheep? (Leicester: Thorpe, Ulverscroft, 2018).*

Eggers, Dave, Thompson, Sunra, Wachter-Boettcher, Sara, Angwin, Julia, Paglen, Trevor and Snowden, Edward J., *The End of Trust: McSweeney's 54* (San Francisco, California: McSweeney's Quarterly Concern, 2018).

Eggers, Dave, *The Circle* (Toronto: Vintage Canada, 2017).

Ferris, Joshua, *Then We Came to the End* (New York: Back Bay Books/Little, Brown and Company, 2017).

Galloway, Alexander R., *The Interface Effect* (Cambridge, UK; Malden, MA: Polity, 2017).

Gere, Cathy, *Pain, Pleasure, and the Greater Good: From the Panopticon to the Skinner Box and Beyond* (Chicago: University of Chicago Press, 2017).

Greenfield, Adam, *Radical Technologies: the Design of Everyday Life* (London & New York: Verso, 2017).

Greif, Mark, *Against Everything: Essays* (New York: Vintage Books, 2017).

Herkenhoff, Paulo, Basilio, Miriam and Maroci, Roxana, eds., *Tempo* (New York: Museum of Modern Art, 2002).

Kholeif, Omar, *Goodbye, World! Looking at Art in the Digital Age* (Berlin: Sternberg Press, 2018).

FURTHER READING

Kivinen, Kati, ed., *Pilvi Takala: Second Shift / Pilvi Takala: Toinen Vuoro* (Helsinki: Garret Publications, 2018).

Ludovico, Alessandro, ed., *UBERMORGEN.COM: Hacking vs. Conceptual Art* (Basel: Christoph Merian Verlag, 2009).

McEwan, Ian, *Machines Like Me* (Toronto: Vintage Canada, 2019).

Melville, Herman, *Bartleby the Scrivener* (Brooklyn, New York: Melville House, 2017).

Miranda, Luis de., *Being and Neonness* (Cambridge: The MIT Press, 2019).

Monem, Nadine Käthe, ed., *Sleeping and Dreaming* (London; Dresden: Black Dog Pub.; Wellcome Collection and Deutsches Hygiene-Museum, 2007).

Neidich, Warren, ed., *Psychopathologies of Cognitive Capitalism: Part Three* (Santa Monica: Ram Publications, 2017).

O'Connell, Mark, *To Be a Machine* (London: Granta, 2018).

O'Shea, Lizzie, *Future Histories: What Ada Lovelace, Tom Paine and the Paris Commune Can Teach Us About Digital Technology* (London & New York: Verso, 2019).

Papadimitriou, Irini, Prescott, Andrew and Rogers, Jon, *Artificially Intelligent* (London: V&A Publishing/Thames & Hudson, 2018).

Parkinson, C. Northcote, *Parkinson's Law* (London: Penguin, 2002).

Cassie McQuater
Black Room, 2017 (p.56)
Online game
cass.itch.io/blackroom
Courtesy of the artist

Viktor IV
Bulgar Time, ca.1982
Metal, glass, quartz mechanism
Private Collection

Garnet Hertz
Phone Safe 2.1, 2019
Custom electronics and steel
Courtesy of the artist

Calm
Sleep Stories: Once Upon a GDPR, 2018
Audio podcast narrated by Peter Jefferson
www.calm.com

JooYoun Paek
Pillowig, 2005
Wearable pillow, digital prints
Courtesy of the artist

Tekja
Awake, 2019
Live data visualisation
Courtesy of the artist
Commissioned by Somerset House with support from the Adonyeva Foundation

Hyphen-Labs
The Gospel According to Yawn, 2019 (p.80)
Digital Interactive Installation
Courtesy of the artist
Commissioned by Somerset House with support from the Adonyeva Foundation

Humans since 1982
A million Times 72v, 2014
White Corian and electronic components
Edition of 82
Courtesy of the artist

FURTHER READING

Phillips, Adam, *Attention Seeking* (London: Penguin, 2019).

Pink, Daniel H., *When* (Edinburgh: Canongate, 2019).

Poitras, Laura et al, *Astro Noise: A Survival Guide to Living Under Total Surveillance* (New York; New Haven; London: Whitney Museum of American Art and Yale University Press, 2016).

Smith, Dominic, *Exceptional Technologies: A Continental Philosophy of Technology* (London: Bloomsbury Academic, 2018).

Sorokin, Vladimir, *The Queue,* trans. Sally Laird (New York: The New York Review of Books, 2011).

Steyerl, Hito, *The Wretched of the Screen* (Berlin: Sternberg Press, 2012).

Thacker, Eugene, *Infinite Resignation* (London: Repeater Books, 2018).

Turkle, Sherry, *Alone Together: Why We Expect More from Technology and Less from Each Other,* (New York: Basic Books, 2017).

Wajcman, Judy, *Pressed for Time* (Chicago: University of Chicago Press, 2014).

Wells, H. G., *The Best Science Fiction Stories of H.G. Wells* (Mineola, New York: Dover Publications, Inc., 2018).

Zamyatin, Yevgeny. *We,* trans. Clarence Brown (New York: Penguin Books, 2014).

EXHIBITION

Curated by Sarah Cook and Somerset House
Lighting Design: Lucy Carter
Associate to Lucy Carter: Sean Gleason
Graphic Design: Europa

Director: Jonathan Reekie
Director of Programmes: Ceri Hand
Head of Exhibition Management: Sophie Clark
Exhibitions Coordinator: Grace Perrett
Technical Production: Thomas Malcherczyk
with Eoin Donnelly
Audio Visual: KS Objectiv

With additional curatorial support from:
Jonathan Powell, Karishma Rafferty and
Stella Sideli

PUBLICATION

24/7: A Wake-up Call for our Non-stop World
Editor: Sarah Cook
Head of Retail: Penelope Wilmott
Publication Coordinator and Production
Manager: Jessica Lowe
Picture Research: Jessica Lowe and
Grace Perrett
Copy editing: Sarah Cook and Anthony Iles
Design: Europa
Printing: Generation Press
Publisher: Somerset House Trust, London

All text © Somerset House Trust and the authors
unless otherwise noted.

ISBN: 978-1-9996154-5-1

The exhibition at Somerset House was made
possible thanks to support from Signify, A/D/O
by MINI, The Adonyeva Foundation, Quebec
Government Office, London, Canada House,
London, Therme Art Program, and the University
of Glasgow.

Thanks also to Somerset House's other official
partners AIAIAI, Omnicolour and L-Acoustics.

Somerset House is grateful to the artists
and lenders to the exhibition as well as all
the contributors to this publication: Douglas
Coupland, Jonathan Crary, Iain Forsyth &
Jane Pollard, Matthew Fuller, Alexandra Daisy
Ginsberg, Ted Hunt, Hyphen-Labs, Inés Cámara
Leret, Esther Leslie, Malcolm McCullough,
Sukhdev Sandhu, Helga Schmid, Sarah Sharma,
Dominic Smith, Tekja, Verso Books and Alan
Warburton.

Every effort has been made to trace the
copyright holders and obtain permission to
reproduce this material. Please do get in touch
with any enquiries or any information relating to
these images or the rights holders.

Published to accompany the exhibition *24/7*
Somerset House, 31 October 2019–23 February, 2020